DESPERATE STAGES   Edward Mullaly

DESPERATE STAGES

New Brunswick's Theatre in the 1840's

Edward Mullaly

Some of the material contained in this book has appeared in different form as articles in *Theatre History In Canada, Nineteenth Century Theatre Research*, and *Studies in Canadian Literature*. The University of New Brunswick has generously provided me with research time and funding. Leads supplied by colleagues in the Association for Canadian Theatre History, especially Ron Bryden, Kathleen Fraser and Mary Elizabeth Smith, have helped me to track down obscure biographical details.

I am particularly grateful to my wife, Laurel Boone, without whose endurance, advice, kindness, and support this project could not have been completed.

Published by Fiddlehead Poetry Books & Goose Lane Editions Ltd., 248 Brunswick Street, Fredericton, New Brunswick, Canada, E3B 1G9, 1987, with the assistance of the Canada Council, the New Brunswick Department of Tourism, Recreation and Heritage, and the University of New Brunswick.

Book design by Julie Scriver
Cover illustration, Charles Freer as "Alonzo the Brave"

All illustrations of Charles Freer appear courtesy of the Billy Rose Theater Collection, New York Public Library at Lincoln Center.
Charles Freer's "Begging Letter" appears courtesy of the Harvrad Theater Collection.

Canadian Cataloguing in Publication Data

Mullaly, Edward, 1941
    Desperate stages

Includes bibliographical references.
ISBN 0-86492-067-9

1. Theater—New Brunswick—History—19th century.
2. Hill, Thomas.   3. Preston, Henry W.   4. Freer, Charles.
PN2305.N4M8 1987   792'.09715   C87-094709-5

Introduction

1845 was a most interesting year in New Brunswick's social and theatrical history. Political values were being questioned as the movement toward Responsible Goverment picked up steam. The foundations of political parties were being laid. Economic attitudes toward the United States were being formed even as the province took its final geographical shape. And a myriad of issues that would concern future generations were being argued vociferously by the editors of the daily and weekly newspapers. One of the editors around whom most, if not all, of these issues swirled was Thomas Hill, editor of the *Loyalist* newspaper, political and social commentator, founder of the Orange Lodge Chapter in Fredericton and, in 1845, a playwright.

Refuge from the political storms buffeting the provincial capital in the winter of 1844-45 was provided to liberals and Tories alike by a meagre troupe of travelling thespians. The actors' world, like the New Brunswick political scene, surged with new laws and fresh sensibilities. In London, the Licensing Act of 1737, which had allowed just two companies the right to perform plays in the city, had lost its effectiveness. By the 1830s, company after company evaded the legal definition of "play" by adding the occasional chord of music or the odd song to their productions, thus, by definition, transforming them from unlicensed plays into legitimate musical entertainments. In the face of such near-universal revolt against the old theatre monopoly, lawmakers passed new regulations in 1843 to legitimize the wide range of saloon and tavern entertainments in east and south London that had been operating on the far fringes of legality for over a century. The tavern music hall, in which the tavern keeper had played host, master of ceremonies, and bouncer, took on a new respectability, as did east-end melodrama. Audience expectations developed accordingly.

South of New Brunswick, American self-awareness was diluting the craving of the previous half century for British stars and the latest London scripts. Audiences gravitated toward plays reflecting their own identity (real or imagined) and American situations. The "Yankee" character found much favor on the east-coast touring circuit—pushing aside the heroes of British high drama—and proclamations of American values began ringing through tragedy and domestic melodrama alike. Even in New England, the condemnation of theatre as the devil's church (or synagogue, depending) was weakening and, at mid-century, fell before such great American morality plays as *Ten Nights in a Bar Room, Uncle Tom's Cabin,* and *The Drunkard.*

In New Brunswick, as in Canada generally, the theatrical situation was less exciting. While American theatre was moving toward self-sufficiency, provincial theatre was more than willing to be nourished with the imported delicacies of the English and American stages. With dramatic appetites sated from such sources, British North Americans seemed little worried by the lack of indigenous theatre and happily wept or cheered in response to the declamation of foreign values mouthed—usually—by foreign actors in foreign plays. This lack of political or social relevance meant that an evening of Fredericton theatre would provide nothing more than a refuge from reality for those whose days were taken up arguing the merits of the Durham Report or sharing the spoils of political patronage. Even royalists such as Thomas Hill, concerned as they were about American influences, welcomed this foreign drama as an escape to a world less spoiled than their own.

Henry W. Preston led his small troupe into Fredericton in December, 1844, having already spent almost two decades touring from the Carolinas to Newfoundland in search of theatrical and financial success. His single formula was to avoid the haunts of his theatrical betters, to establish himself in a district that offered no theatrical competition, and then to tour to the surrounding towns in order to enlarge his audience. It was a strategy that seldom worked. But, in doggedly following this plan, Preston himself was part of a larger pattern. Like other British thespians who had heard the Siren call to success in America, he had first attempted to establish himself as an actor. When he realized that managers were not clamoring to employ his theatrical skills, he was left with the option of employing himself. Lacking the financial resources to set himself up as a theatrical manager in a large centre, he could only turn to "the provinces." As with dozens of his compatriots, his fate was determined on the fringes of that theatrical world to which he felt himself drawn, and from which he was unable to turn away.

Henry Preston's failure provides a microcosm of the actor-manager's world at mid-century. Similarly, the wanderings that brought the English actor Charles Freer from the London stages to work for Preston in Saint John and Fredericton in 1845 provide a template of the day-to-day life of a mediocre actor who, unable to find favor on the more demanding stages of west London, had achieved a modest reputation on the east-London stages, who then followed the path of his more talented contemporaries such as George Frederick Cooke, Edmund Kean, and Charles Macready to the golden shores of the new world, who quickly and painfully discovered that the fires of audience enthusiasm burned but weakly for him, and who was left with the more basic goal of avoiding starvation.

This continued commitment to theatre by Preston and Freer in the face of consistent failure is impossible to rationalize. Yet tale after melancholic tale in the theatrical pages of the times show that, like moths to the lamp, second-rate actors and managers remained attracted to a trade at which their own inadequacies could bring them nothing but failure and poverty. Preston's and Freer's own lack of success is not explained by the similar failure of others, but the larger pattern serves as a context in which to view the contributions of individuals such as these two, who provided the base upon which their more successful confrères built their prosperity.

All three of these individuals whose lives intersected in 1845 in Fredericton—Thomas Hill the Tory newspaperman, Henry Preston the actor-manager, and Charles Freer the would-be star—failed to achieve those goals toward which they had directed their lives. Curiously, none of the three seems ever to have thought of changing his goals. This is a fact for which there is no other explanation than that each believed mightily in the hopes to which he had committed himself. The interweaving of these three lives creates a whole that is larger than the sum of its parts. Personal decisions which on the surface seem to lack any complexity whatever, such as the playwright's choice of topic for a play or the actor's choice of play for a benefit performance, are complex amalgams of political, theatrical and personal biases. The arrival or departure of a particular actor, apparently due to coincidence, is either the end or the beginning of an action which reflects on, and is a reflection of, not only a personal career, but the theatrical state of the times. The response to a particular production, likewise, depends not merely on the performance itself but on the personal and political wars raging between its producer, the actors, and journalistic critics unwilling to leave their politics aside.

This narrative is an attempt both to explore a theatrical world by studying the personalities involved in it and to illustrate the more general truth that seldom is history so simple that it can be reduced to mere dates or facts.

Chapter One

'Tis duty that calls us, and we will obey;
'Tis the deep debt of gratitude bids us to say
That the "Loyalist" paper deserves us to fill
Our Glasses, and drink to the health of T. Hill.

When warm-hearted Neth'ry was attacked by Boors,
The blood-thirsty villains, who surrounded his doors,
When the cowardly Mayor did not dare interpose,
To protect worthy men from such devilish foes.

And, when villains of every grade and degree,
From the midnight assassin to him who takes "fee,"
Were assiduously trying, each in his own way,
The flag of rebellion aloft to display,

It was then Doak & Hill forth fearlessly came,
In the might and the pow'r of Conservative fame,
Expos'd the dark deeds of the disloyal crew
And *proved* that the "Loyalist" is a "true blue."

Tho' incarcerated as others have been,
The victims of malice, injustice and spleen,
Yet unflinching integrity still they held fast,
Their flag; like brave Nelson, they "nail'd to the mast."

Their "Standard" is rais'd, near "Head Quarters" it stands,
Come boys rally 'round it with hearts and with hands
That ne'er will relinquish the glorious strife
Of war, with the foe that would sap Saxon life.

Come boys, rally 'round it with "three British cheers."
And ne'er be dismay'd till the "Loyalist" fears!
'Till then we may safely expect to retain
The hope, that New Brunswick her rights will attain.

So now to the "Loyalist"—loyal and true
We tender our praise, as all patriots do;
O long may it flourish our birth right to screen—
Three cheers for the Loyalist, and nine for the Queen.

J.G.L.
[John G. Lorimer?]

The Constitutional Lyrist, Doak and Hill eds. (Fredericton, 1845), 230-33.

❧

Fredericton, New Brunswick, was never the intended destination of the horde of nineteenth-century British playwrights and actors who saw America as a land flowing with milk and money. Yet in that town of 4000 people, in the mid-1840s, the theatrical paths of three individuals crossed: a Tory newspaper editor who can be considered a playwright only if his single political satire is sufficient to give him that title, an expatriate Irishman who had changed his name and committed his life to an unsuccessful theatrical vocation as an actor-manager, and an east-end London stage favorite who would have declared himself by choice an actor and only by grim necessity a company manager. The deaths of all three at the end of the next decade—by suicide in the case of the two actors, and the Fredericton editor by sudden sickness in near-friendless poverty—closed out lives which are much more interesting and important for their failures than for any passing victories. The three would never enjoy more success than they salvaged from their 1844-45 failures, as the Tory editor was thrown in jail by the provincial legislature, the actor-manager was forced to flee Fredericton one step ahead of the bailiff, and the London actor lost forever the opportunity to play the great tragic roles he had assayed at the pinnacle of his career. In a way, temporary success was responsible for their later failures, for it gave to each an earnest of a future which was not to be.

Of the three, the newspaper editor Thomas Hill came to Fredericton first. For a man whose writing career was spent exploring events and ideas through the editorial columns of newspapers, Hill gave his readers surprisingly little information about his own background. Throughout the 1840s, he airily dismissed accusations concerning his past rather than

10

marshalling the evidence necessary to disprove them. He ignored editorial innuendoes that he was a bigamist. He shrugged off questions concerning his recent American loyalties and, when publically attacked for irresponsibility, drunkeness and disregard of honest debts, he simply hurled the accusations back on his tormentors. Not until 1858, when forced to do so during a libel case on which he had staked his whole future, did he attempt to defend his good name. But, by then, it was too late.[1]

At that trial, Hill testified that he had been born in Cornwall, England, in 1807. Early in 1831 he sailed from Plymouth to Quebec City. After four years in Quebec, which he presumably spent at his carpenter's trade, he moved to Grand Falls, New Brunswick, where Sir John Caldwell hired him for the summer. Next, he travelled further south to Woodstock, and then west and south across the border to Bangor, Maine. He worked there for about a year before moving to Orono, where he and his family remained from June, 1836, until 1839. In December, 1839, he packed his tools, left his wife and children, and came back across the border to New Brunswick, where he spent the rest of his life. No one questioned these early dates provided by Hill; the 1858 trial examined not the event, but rather the motive for Hill's move to New Brunswick. The two sources of information on this subject—Hill's friends and Hill's enemies—are equally unreliable.

In any case, Woodstock, where he practiced his craft and developed a reputation as a musician, a writer of songs, and a wood carver, remained Hill's home for only a year and a half. He then moved down to Saint John where, presumably, he started out once more as a carpenter. In the summer of 1842, he decided to begin a new penny paper, the *Aurora,* which would be published three times a week. The address for this paper, Robertson's Building, at the corner of Market Square and Water Street, was the home of printer James Doak's *Loyalist* newspaper, and the obvious inference is that Hill was one of the several Saint John editors who made use of Doak's press. The *Aurora* first appeared on September 12, 1842. According to the *New Brunswick Courier*'s editor Henry Chubb, Hill's paper was "neatly printed, and . . . altogether respectably got up, and will doubtless come in for a fair share of public patronage."[2] No copies have survived. According to Hill, it was to be an unprejudiced political and literary paper, but, despite these high ideals, it lasted less than a year. George Fenety, never a friend to Hill, summed up the *Aurora*'s history by saying its editor "had not brains enough to keep it afloat, and so it went down."[3]

The *Aurora* quietly passed away, but its editor, left in a state of "utter destitution and wretchedness,"[4] was thrown in jail for debt. Fortunately for Hill, he had become friends with James Doak, whose *Loyalist* was proving to be a much more successful paper. Both men looked upon Responsible Government as a dangerous Whig scheme, and the forces of liberalism as their main antagonists; they were willing to fight against all who were enemies to the Protestant religion; and both viewed Orangeism as the bulwark of the Protestant faith. Sharing such principles, the *Loyalist* owner not only paid Hill's debts and got him out of jail, but endowed his failed and penniless compatriot with decent garments and the editorship of his paper. Such an arrangement assured Doak that his paper would hold to the conservative and Protestant course he had charted and freed him to concentrate on the printing side of his business, but he would have much cause to regret this charitable act. Hill's reputation as an irresponsible wanderer and a vicious imbiber, loyal only to his life of dissipation, was, unfortunately, not entirely a fiction created by his enemies. Over the next three years, the partnership between Doak and Hill would be dissolved at least four times on account of Hill's antisocial habits. Each time, the long-suffering Doak took Hill back to carry on the offensive against their common foes.

The *Loyalist* had two main enemies in Saint John: the *Mirror* and the *Morning News*. The former newspaper was the shorter-lived of the two, surviving only until 1843. Hill looked upon it as little more than "an organ of sedition," got up to promulgate the Catholic faith and the sayings of Daniel O'Connell, "the leather lunged vendor of scurrility and anarchy."[5] The feud between the *Loyalist* and the *Morning News* was much more serious. George Fenety had begun the *Morning News* at the end of the previous decade, and he remained its editor until he was appointed Queen's Printer in 1863. He and his paper were among the dominant Saint John voices promulgating Liberalism and Responsible Government, and thus they were on the receiving end of regular editorial vituperation from the *Loyalist* editors.

On May 4, 1843, after the *Loyalist* completed its first year in Saint John, Hill announced that its editorial offices were about to be relocated to Fredericton, to a "building lately occupied by Mr. H. Sutherland, Queen St., immediately over Mr. Cummings' store."[6] The purpose of the move was to situate the editors closer to the heat of the Legislative kitchen, where they would continue to defend those values which provided the paper with its philosophical foundations. A farewell editorial in what Hill occasionally called "Fenerty's Morning News-*ance*" warned Fredericton, and especially its Sheriff, what to expect. "Mr. Gill," Fenety wrote, was a man more acquainted with a jail than a printing office, possessed more of impudence than common sense, and composed more of brass than of honor.[7] Fenety ended his catalogue of Hill's imperfections with one of the few physical references to Hill ever to appear in print:

> We do remember . . . he had a remarkable head of hair; it seemed as if all the combing it had ever got, was by scratching; his general appearance [was] rather greasy; but this is not to be wondered at, being a very slippery fellow in his dealings, it would be a miracle if he did not give evidence of it in his looks. We should have examined him more minutely at the time, did we think we would ever have occasion to *advertise* him; having no such suspicion, we passed him by as we would any other *compost heap*, too loathsome for closer observation.[8]

Soon after the *Loyalist* began publishing in Fredericton, Hill responded to this character assassination with remarkable restraint. He dismissed "Fenerty's" accusations as "the splenetic excrescence of a jaundiced mind"; he hinted at Fenety's own past "in one of the gambling hells of New Orleans"; he observed that the *Morning News* editor, "lacking the talents necessary to furnish a paper which should be read by the upper and middling classes of society . . . has pandered to the tastes of the vicious and corrupted; and among them his paper obtains its principal circulation"; and he concluded that suing Fenety for libel would be "a work of supererogation" since "it would be impossible to get anything from him but his hide, and asses are too plentiful now-a-day for their hides to be worth much."[9]

The move to Fredericton brought changes to the paper. It became the *Loyalist and Conservative Advocate*. Hill's name appeared, for the first time, with Doak's as co-publisher. Its literary content increased, the front page being taken over by serialized stories and novels written anonymously "for the *Loyalist*." It would be difficult to imagine that this fiction, with its New Brunswick settings, its narrative blended with original poetry and songs, and its strongly loyalist plots and themes, was written by anyone other than Hill. The change of cities, however, did nothing to lessen Hill's belligerence toward other editors. In his first editorial, following a disclaimer beginning "We detest egotism," Hill lashed out at his competition.[10] He attacked Fenety as a liar and an untalented editor. Although he found it difficult to criticize James Philips, publisher of *Head Quarters*, since that Fredericton newspaper had published only its prospectus, Hill felt obliged to point out that an editor "whose character is spotless seldom *boasts* of it." Even the literary *Amaranth* was castigated for allowing its high standards to fall off.

Hill's attention soon focussed on two targets: Lemuel A. Wilmot, a member of the Assembly; and Ned Ward, editor of the Fredericton *Sentinel*. According to Hill, Ward was little more than the "trencher-licker at Government House."[11] And, when it appeared that Ward's *Sentinel* would fold before the end of the year, Hill published a satirical dialogue hinting broadly that Ward had lost his previous post of Queen's Printer in Bermuda because of his monomaniacal lying. Ward rose to the bait, denied the allegation, and challenged Hill to produce any evidence he might have. Hill welcomed the opportunity to embarrass "Sir John Harvey's principal toady," and published the pertinent documents at length. Stung, Ward toured the Woodstock area and investigated the rumors concerning Hill's past that had been drifting up and down the Saint John river valley since Hill had appeared there on Christmas day, 1839. In January, 1844, Ward joined Fenety in the attack on Hill's politics and private life. He wrote:

> Since the establishment of the *Loyalist* in this place, it has each week teemed with falsehoods, against every public character, who is opposed to the old system of colonial misrule, that manifested no ordinary degree of invention, on the one hand; or supposed credulity and ignorance, to believe them on the other. . . . As to the character whose name is obtruded upon the public notice, as the Editor; an opinion certainly is current, that he is an American deserter; and there are persons here, who think he would be worth thirty dollars to them, if they had him at Houlton. While at Woodstock we made enquiry with reference to this individual, who resided there for some time; and learnt that if he did not run away from the American army, in a moral

14

and humane point of view he did worse—he came away from his wife and destitute family, whom he left in the United States, to be maintained by strangers; and where we believe they are at present supported by parochial relief.[12]

To Fenety's innuendoes that Hill was an incompetent editor branded with a criminal record, Ward had added the direct accusations that Hill was a liar; that, although he wrapped himself in the British mantle, he had taken a soldier's oath of allegiance to America; and that he had left his wife and babes to fend for themselves in Maine. The first of Ward's accusations was political rhetoric. The third was true, and in fact it embarrassed Hill when he remarried in New Brunswick. But the second accusation, to which Ward returned again and again, and to which Hill's only response was that Ward was a "dunce" who should have invented a fabrication "not so easily contradicted,"[13] would provide the background for Hill's editorial downfall in the next decade.

Ward promised further revelations concerning "the Editor of the Loyalist who passes under the name of *Hill*." This persiflage was sidetracked, however, as the forces of law and order descended on the *Loyalist* editors and threw them into jail for Hill's slanderous attacks on members of the legislature, and also by a fire in the *Sentinel's* offices—a fire that, the *Loyalist* speculated, Ward himself had set.[14] Ward considered the charge of arson to be a slander so serious that it could be answered by criminal prosecution of the *Loyalist*. In order not to prejudice his potential suit, Ward did not follow through on his promise to publish more of the Woodstock rumors about Hill, but his threat of legal action remained as empty as most of the editorial sabre-rattling in the warring newspapers. By March, 1844, the *Sentinel* was once more illuminating the *Loyalist* editor's character, this time for daring to impugn the drinking and sexual habits of a touring Temperance lecturer:

That rum-drinking and rum-selling should be defended in such a quarter is not surprising, considering whence arises much of its support; but that a false imputation of an irregular life and a disregard of conjugal ties, should be adduced against an innocent man, by a fellow who left his wife and family to starve in another land, or to be supported by the precarious bounty of strangers, where they may now be perishing for aught he knows, and who for months was the inmate of a house of ill-fame, and formed part of its *"materiel"*. . . .[15]

❦ NEW-BRUNSWICK GIRLS ❧
Air—Jessy o' Dumblane.

COME fill the glass cheerly—a bumper o' kindness,
   To the fair of New-Brunswick, whom none can excel;
For surely his eyes must be stricken with blindness,
   Who'd a stranger prefer to a New-Brunswick belle.
They're blooming and fair—void of showy refining—
   And pure as the heavens which o'er them unfurls;
Their beauty and goodness so sweetly entwining—
   No heart but must worship our New-Brunswick Girls.

The fair of Italia, so witty and sprightly,
   Are fickle, and often prove false to their lords,
While the ladies of Spain, whose black eyes shine so
       brightly,
   Must sometimes be won by their lovers keen swords,
And the famed belles of France, though they've all that
       can varnish,
   Voluptuously clasp'd, in the giddy waltz whirls;
But waltz nor fandango, nor aught that can tarnish,
   Shall e'er fix a stain on our New-Brunswick Girls.
Here are blonds and brunettes—here is ev'ry
       complexion,
   From the maid of Glendower to th' Saxon or Dane;
All duteous and kind, such unbounded affection,
   That search the world through you'll ne'er find it
       again.
If e'er they once love you, though trouble o'ertakes
       you—
   Though poverty on you its thunderbolt hurls—
Though blighted and seared, they will never forsake
       you—
   May heaven still bless them, our New-Brunswick Girls.

T. Hill

The Constitutional Lyrist, 232-33.

❧

16

Such crimination adds little to the biographical material already published by Ward, except for the intriguing accusation that Hill had formed part of the "materiel" of a brothel. Further unsupported rumors about Hill's past picked up in Woodstock would undoubtedly have continued to find their embroidered way into Ward's columns if the *Sentinel* had not gone out of business that spring. Hill's brief obituary for the *Sentinel* castigated it as an "ultra-radical abortion of a foul brain and a jaundiced heart" and its editor as a mere "hired tool of Sir John Harvey."[16]

Many of these accusations concerning Hill's character and background were little more than the customary smear tactics of editors wishing to crush their opponent's cause by crushing their opponent. But the charge that kept coming back concerned Hill's enlistment in—and desertion from—the American army. The *Loyalist's* masthead proclaimed the paper to be the "Conservative Advocate," and its motto declared "All I wish is to serve my country." If the author of such sentiments had joined the American army he would have had to forswear his British allegiance. The insinuation was that not only had Hill betrayed his British values but that in deserting from the American army at Houlton he had also betrayed his newly-acquired American loyalties. Whether truth or slander, such hints of hypocrisy were useful to the *Morning News* and the *Sentinel* in their defense of Responsible Government against the attacks of the ultra-Royalist Hill.

The accusation that he was a deserter came at Hill from all sides in 1844. The editors of *Head Quarters*, whose prospectus Hill had so facilely criticized in his first Fredericton *Loyalist*, would not let the issue die down. A delicate song of character assassination appearing in its columns began:

O who'd a thought when Tommy Gill
    Listed a Yankee sodger,
And walked his tracks on Houlton hill
    A blue and yellow codger,
That in a British Province he
    His uniform would barter,
And that his Sally'd live to see
    Him git a Magna Charter.
Chorus:
Yankee Doodle keep it up
Yankee Doodle crickey,

Yankee Doodle shout for Tom
And plague take Mother Dickey.

I'm glad Tom douced his Yankee gun
    And turn'd a blue nose Tory.
He might a stayed till time was done
    In Yankee land before he
Could make the Gustay Congress bleed
    But now he's done it smarter;
He's made each ditch a Runnimede
    And got a Magna Charter.
Chorus:
Yankee doodle, &c.[17]

This parody of "Yankee Doodle" bit deeper because Hill was known for both his musical ability and his facility in adapting his own poems to existing tunes. When asked later why he did not sue *Head Quarters* for libel, he responded that he "thought a man would make nothing by prosecuting the author of a doggerel rhyme."[18] A second possible reason for Hill's refusal to prosecute might have been that the accusation was true. The early acts of Hill's Fredericton drama depended little on this particular plot, but when his life turned to tragedy, fourteen years later, the final scenes would focus almost entirely on his negligent attitude toward this recurring charge of desertion.

Less than a year after moving to Fredericton, and while he was still exchanging editorial barbs with Ned Ward, Hill managed the greatest triumph of his career, a drama in which he held the stage as a protagonist fighting for freedom and justice. But the villain of the piece had little in common with those appearing on the Fredericton stage—it was the House of Assembly.

The question of freedom of the press had first arisen in the province in the previous century. In 1784, two editors were indicted before a Maugerville Grand Jury for attacking the government's methods of granting land and relief to the Loyalists. A year later, an unfortunate individual named George Handyside was heard to utter strong criticism against the government. He "was summoned before the bar of the House of Assembly, found guilty, and forced to kneel and apologize without having had recourse to the courts."[19] A more notorious example of this practice occurred in 1837, when the editor of the Miramichi *Gleaner*, John A. Pierce, characterized L.A.

Wilmot's accusations against him on the floor of the Assembly as having been made with that member's "usual effrontery and disregard for truth."[20] Editor Pierce was brought before the bar and then, upon orders of the Assembly, was effectively silenced by being jailed until the end of the session.

The case involving the *Loyalist* was remarkably similar. In the session of 1844, a resolution was passed supporting the Governor General of Canada, Sir Charles Metcalfe, "a person," according to James Hannay, "who is said to have much ability, but who was certainly unfit for the position he occupied."[21] The resolution, of which Hill approved, supported Sir Charles in maintaining the prerogatives of the Crown in matters of provincial Royal appointments—a right without which, from the perspective of Hill and many others in New Brunswick, monarchical institutions in Canada would most surely be weakened. Opposition to this resolution was opposition to strong Loyalist ties with England. And while the notion of Responsible Government received but little acceptance in the New Brunswick Assembly of 1844, Hill was ready to attack any elected representative who publicly proclaimed such an anti-royalist sentiment. Nowhere did the *Loyalist* editor find the spirit of British loyalty more lacking than in the breast of L.A. Wilmot. Wilmot was only one of eleven who voted against the resolution supporting the Governor General, but Hill rightly saw him as a leader of the small group of members who would like to move the Assembly in directions suggested by the Durham Report. Not only did Hill attack Wilmot for his liberal political views but he excoriated the member for York for his lack of personal integrity.

Hill's most virulent editorial against Wilmot provoked the Assembly into a course of action that would change forever the relationship between the Assembly and the New Brunswick press. Wilmot was accused not only of being "hostile alike to British supremacy, British laws, and those in whose veins runs the warm current of British blood," but also of avowing himself the friend of the Canadian rebels, and

> [stating] what was absolutely false and unfounded concerning the oppression of the French race by the British . . . and [giving] the lie to the Governor General! . . . But this is not the most disgraceful part of his conduct. After having been distinctly charged with the assertions he had made by no less than *five* members of the House, what does he do? Why turns round and

19

denies point blank that he ever made use of the expressions, although he had repeated the words with the strongest emphasis some half dozen times! . . . and lacking the moral courage to face the matter out with his constituents, the poltroon, screening himself from all the responsibility a *true gentleman* feels, under the plea of being an anti-duelist, he had the impudence to tell the members of the House that their ears had deceived them.[22]

An editorial denouncing Wilmot as a liar, a coward and a hypocrite might have been thought a little excessive by the Assembly, although such a description was scarcely less complimentary than the Saint John *Chronicle*'s characterization of Wilmot as "that inflated bag of wind."[23] In fact, many Assemblymen would have agreed with the *Loyalist*'s sentiments, if not with Hill's expression of them, had Hill's harangue stopped within such acceptable limits. But his diatribe continued, building toward its final image of Wilmot as a "hound" who crept into the confidence of the voters of York county "and then bit the hand which fed him." The editor's final hope was that the electors would tell him "they have no further need of his services—that being loyal themselves they will no longer be represented by a rebel and a coward, and drive him back to the kennel, from which he emerged to poison with his fetid breath the atmosphere of New Brunswick."

The viciousness of this editorial's ending—coupled with Hill's effrontery in having copies of the paper delivered to every Assemblyman's desk—was too much even for Wilmot's enemies. Reformers and Torys alike agreed that the *Loyalist* must be silenced. Hill and Doak were, in the tradition of Handyside and Pierce before them, called before the bar of the House of Assembly for Breach of Privilege. They admitted responsibility for the editorial, and the Assembly instantly threw them in jail "there to remain during pleasure."[24] The press was free, the Assembly concluded, but not as free as all that.

Whereas other editors had accepted their fate without legal battle, Hill and Doak appealed to the court for release on a writ of *habeas corpus*, arguing that the Legislature had acted "in direct contradiction to the Home Government, whose instructions were before them in the words 'The power of arrest does not extend to Colonial Legislation.'"[25] Judge Carter accepted their argument and granted their writ. The Assembly was free to make whatever laws it wished, but only the courts had the right to enforce them. The freed editor and publisher went immediately to the House to bait its members with their freedom, hurried back to their office, and quickly brought forth an unrepentant issue of the *Loyalist*.

The Assembly immediately began a debate on the matter of their own House privileges, with some members wondering now if they had any to debate. In the grand parliamentary tradition, they decided to form a committee to look into the matter. This committee, chaired by John Allan, reported back to the House in late March that on the basis of "usage" and "necessary incident" the Legislature had the right to do what the Courts had just told them they had no right to do.[26] Allan's report was debated at great length, and with a noticeable lack of unanimity. "For several hours there was a confusion of tongues, such a noise (remarked a correspondent at the time,) as had never been heard since the uproar among the workmen in rearing the walls of Babel."[27] Not only was there nothing the Assembly could legally do to punish the editors, but the law-makers were obliged to vote Hill and Doak the sum of fifty pounds for covering the Session in their paper. Adding a final insult, the *Loyalist*'s proprietors sued the Speaker and the Sergeant-at-Arms for false arrest and were awarded roughly two hundred and fifty pounds. Hill and Doak had brought the Assembly's custom of jailing its editorial critics at whim forever to an end.

While the battle had been one of principle, it had also been one of party. Hill was a Tory "of an extreme type,"[28] and L.A. Wilmot, who "had been charged with radicalism, republican-ism, and rebellion, for advocating the views propounded in the Durham Report,"[29] was one of only a few liberals raising the cry of Responsible Government in the provincial Assembly. Although the House was not willing to spring further to the defense of a member with such radical ideas, the party newspapers were. Thus Hill found himself lambasted by the same fourth estate whose freedoms he had just secured. Ward, in his Fredericton *Sentinel*, characterized the incident as a "vulgar and virulent attack upon a gentleman . . . originating in the basest of motives—a desire to pander to the depraved tastes, and to gratify the malevolent designs of others."[30] The journalistic voice of liberalism in Saint John, the *Morning News*, mischievously added a religious level to the situation by pointing out that those who would support Hill must do so quietly for fear of offending their Catholic neighbors.[31]

Hill had always extolled the values of Protestantism and the Orange Order, defending both for loyalty to the Sovereign, reverence towards the word of God, orderliness, and tolerance in religious matters. Unfortunately for the people of Woodstock, Fredericton and Saint John, these ideal qualities would become heavily infused with political, patriotic and personal animosities before the end of the decade, and the peaceful Orange Parades of July 12 would give way to scenes of riot and disorder as Catholics and Protestants clashed in the streets. But, in the years immediately before this violence, Hill had attended meetings of the Orange Lodge in Saint John and was impressed with the values and civil spirit he saw in the organization. On July 5, 1844, he founded the Graham Chapter of the Orange Lodge in Fredericton. While the Orange Lodge figures centrally in the political development of the province, Hill's editorials suggest that he saw it less as a political institution than as an embodiment of those British principles he held dear. In fact, his later marriage to a Catholic girl named McDowell proves that personal ideals and not politics or bigotry were behind his zeal for the fraternity. He may well have been wrong in his interpretation of Orangism, but he was not untrue to himself.

A similar charge of inconsistency could emerge from Hill's drinking problems. The Orange Lodge he founded conformed to the widely-approved standard of Total Abstinence, and in the editorial pages of the *Loyalist* Hill defended the mores of the provincial Total Abstinence societies. Yet the *Loyalist* editor was widely known for his personal commitment to rum-drinking. Hill's battle earlier in the year with the Assembly showed how strongly he could fight for a matter of principle, and perhaps no one would be more able to recognize the virtue of abstinence than a person unable to practice it. The tavern owned by Hill's mother-in-law, while not a factor in his espousal of Orange precepts, surely provided him with opportunity to meditate on the potentially salubrious effects of sobriety. In this sense, Hill's recognition of the abstinence ideal while drinking to excess is no more hypocritical than his acceptance of the Orange values of loyalty, reverence and tolerance while marrying a Catholic.

Adding still another facet to Hill's personal complexity is his creative side. While it is unusual to find such a combative man writing poetry of any kind, it is more surprising to find, tucked away in the various corners of the *Loyalist*, peaceful, escapist poems and songs modestly signed "T. Hill." In Fredericton and Saint John "public dinners and convivial gatherings rang to the verses of Thomas Hill."[32] Hill collected some of these verses in an 1845 volume published by the *Loyalist*, entitled *The Constitutional Lyrist*. Others verses found their way into Hill's 1850 compilation, *A Book of Orange Songs*. His poems are celebrations of patriotism, Christmas, and other sentiments far from the immediate world of party politics. The longest of these poems, written in July 1844, covered the entire first page of the *Loyalist* and part of the second.[33] Entitled "What is Life?" it explores, in an unexpectedly naive and innocent fashion, the poet's asking of that eternal question at all stages of life. The poet asks it finally of an ancient, dying man:

He gazed—words came to his relief—
His voice was thick, his answer brief:
"'Tis, when with age and sorrows bent,
To look back on a life well-spent—
'Tis, when afflicted by his rod,
To joy to meet a pard'ning God!
To draw o'er other's faults a blot,
And be contented with your lot.
To part from all below in love,
And hope for happiness above!"
He paused — I gazed upon the clay;
But as the spirit passed away,
Methought I heard a voice from Heaven
Sing—"*This is life—to be forgiven!*"

The accusation of later critics that Hill was a man utterly inconsistent with himself suggests that they had cast him in a rather narrow mould and were unwilling to have him step beyond it. Hill's turbulent editorials and his romantic poetry, taken together, demonstrate not inconsistency, but single-minded stubborn idealism applied to every aspect of life. Like the romantic stage heroes of his day, Hill's life embraced these ambiguities. In fact, Hill was constantly aware of his position on the public stage. His columns ring with the same melodramatic rhythms that playgoers heard in the great moral lectures which passed for mid-nineteenth century theatre. With the emotional hyperbole of Sheridan's Rolla and the moral fervor of Addison's Cato, Hill carried himself through his editorial columns as the champion of justice and truth. Unfortunately, he also shared the myopia of those tragic heroes in his blind commitment to righteous causes. His shield was conservativism, his sword his editorial columns, and his tragic flaw his excessive championing of British patriotism against the less heroic and more democratic notion of Responsible Government.

With Ned Ward out of the newspaper business, and his suits against the Assembly resolved in his favour, Hill's columns in the fall of 1844 turned to more peaceful matters. In September, he wrote of the pleasures of attending the circus which had recently arrived in Fredericton. Later that month, he attended a musical concert in Saint John. In October, he visited Sussex. In November, he again travelled to Saint John. Even the appearance of new competition, the *New Brunswick Reporter* edited by James Hogg, did not summon Hill to the barricades. His criticism that Hogg's paper was half liberal, while James Phillips' *Head Quarters* was whole hog in that direction, was more playful than belligerent. Autumn, 1844, was a tranquil season for Hill. And then, in December, a penniless actor-manager named Henry Preston and the sorry remnants of his travelling troupe found their way to Fredericton.

✍ *ANNIVERSARY SONG,* ✍
For the Twelfth day of July, and sung in St. John, July 12th, 1844

YE Orangemen of Brunswick
 Who make this grand display,
And congregate this Glorious Twelfth
 To celebrate the day.
Since Popery was this day o'erthrown
 All Protestants should join,
   And each voice
   Shall rejoice
That King William crossed the Boyne—
That the bigot's reign this day was closed
When William cross'd the Boyne.

'Twas on the walls of Derry
  The prentice boys did bleed,
When "No Surrender" was their cry
  And Walker did them lead.
But William Prince of Orange came,
  And soon broke through their lines,
      And he stood
      The iron flood
  When his army cross'd the Boyne—
When he gallantly led on the van
  To vict'ry o'er the Boyne.

Cheer up, our cause is gaining,
  Lo, Ulster takes the van!
Th' obnoxious Act's expiring,
  And humbled is old Dan.
Whilst here New-Brunswick's sons press on
  The Orange ranks to join,
      And they dare
      Each breast to bear,
  For the colours of the Boyne—
Who would not die 'neath Britain's flag
  And the colours of the Boyne.

This Glorious Anniversary
  Each Protestant should hail,
For freed were they from Popery
  When James's host turn'd tail.
Long as the Union Jack shall last,
  Or loyal men combine,
      Heart and hand
      Shall each band
  Pledge "the Hero of the Boyne"—
Pledge the memory of the Noble Prince
  Who conquered at the Boyne.

T. Hill

The Constitutional Lyrist, 134-35

Notes

1. There are three main accounts of Hill's 1858 trial against the *New Brunswick Reporter* for publishing a libel: the *New Brunswick Reporter and Fredericton Advertiser,* March 5, 12, and 19; the *Carleton Sentinel,* March 6 and April 10; and the *Head Quarters,* March 17 and 24. While newspapers may sometimes be thought to provide unbiased accounts of events, it is difficult to ignore the fact that in this case the *Reporter's* editor, James Hogg, was the defendant and the *Head Quarters'* editor, Thomas Hill, was the plaintiff. Hill wrote the *Head Quarters'* account himself.
2. *Courier,* September 17, 1842.
3. *Morning News,* May 31, 1843.
4. *Loyalist,* March 12, 1846.
5. *Loyalist,* April 20, 1843.
6. *Loyalist,* May 25, 1843.
7. *Morning News,* May 31, 1843.
8. *Morning News,* May 31, 1843
9. *Loyalist,* June 5, 1843.
10. *Loyalist,* May 25, 1843.
11. *Loyalist,* August 31, 1843.
12. *Sentinel,* January 26, 1844. Also known as the *Sentinel Advertiser.*
13. *Loyalist,* January 18, 1844.
14. *Sentinel Advertiser,* February 2, 1844.
15. *Sentinel,* March 22, 1844.
16. *Loyalist,* April 25, 1844.
17. Quoted in the *Reporter,* March 12, 1858.
18. Quoted in *Head Quarters,* March 24, 1858.
19. J.R. Harper, *Historical Dictionary of New Brunswick Newspapers and Periodicals* (Fredericton: University of New Brunswick, 1961), xv.
20. W.S. MacNutt, *New Brunswick: A History: 1784-1867* (Toronto: MacMillan, 1963), 251.
21. James Hannay, *History of New Brunswick* (Saint John: John A. Bowes, 1909), II, 88.
22. *Loyalist,* February 23, 1844.
23. Quoted in MacNutt, 265.
24. *Journal of the House of Assembly of New Brunswick 1844,* 110.
25. *Loyalist,* February 28, 1844.
26. *Journal,* 231-40.
27. G.E. Fenety, *Political Notes and Observations* (Fredericton: S.R. Miller, 1867), 98.

28. Hannay, II, 97.
29. MacNutt, 287.
30. *Sentinel,* March 8, 1844.
31. *Morning News,* March 8, 1844.
32. MacNutt, 316.
33. *Loyalist,* July 25, 1844.

Chapter Two

Henry W. Preston, the actor-manager who found his way to Fredericton in December 1844, had much in common with Thomas Hill. Both were immigrants to America. Hill had come out from England in 1831 and had worked his way south from Quebec City. Preston came out from Ireland in the late 1820s and had acted his way north from the southern United States. Neither had made any money. Both were living alone: Hill had deserted his wife in Maine a few years earlier, and Preston's wife had recently abandoned him and his troupe while they struggled for survival in Newfoundland. Most importantly, though Hill's writing and Preston's acting had kept both men in near-penury, neither would deviate from his vocation.

Originally an Irish hatter named Patrick Hoy, Henry W. Preston probably began his North American career sometime in the mid-1820s.[1] By 1828 he had come to America, attempted to establish himself as an actor, and married a woman named Baker, from Sing Sing, New York.[2] Over the next seven years, their theatrical travels took them from the southern states to Canada. On December 31, 1828, Mrs Preston made her New York debut at a minor theatre, the Lafayette, playing Young Norval in John Home's popular *Douglas*. At its *premiere* in Edinburgh in 1756, this great Scottish melodrama had inspired a proud voice from the pit to exclaim "Whaur's yer Willy Shakespeare noo?"[3] But Mrs Preston's New Year's Eve debut in the theatrical centre of the New World evoked no such emotional outpouring. Instead, the couple was forced to continue the life of wandering actors, choosing engagements either together or separately as their pocketbooks demanded. Sixteen months later, in April 1830, the couple were invited to Fayetteville, North Carolina, by the local Thalian Association, to add a level of professionalism to their amateur productions. The *Carolina Observer* announced that a benefit performance of another old theatrical warhorse, *The Honey Moon*, for Mrs Preston would be followed by a recitation by Preston himself.[4] A letter which appeared in the *Carolina Observer* suggests that

Mrs Preston's acting talents drew more attention than those of her husband, and also that both their efforts were doomed to failure: "The neat and beautiful style in which the Theatre has been repaired, the exertions of the Association to induce Actors of eminence to perform for the gratification of the Public, and the repeated evidence of Mrs Preston's talents in her profession, call loudly for a more liberal display of patronage. . ." Unfortunately, the call went unanswered, and the Prestons were forced to move on.

The touring Prestons must have crossed paths with Vincent DeCamp, who was active in South Carolina in 1830, for DeCamp hired them, along with other actors who were in the Carolinas at the same time, for his 1831 summer season in Montreal.[5] DeCamp, by this time, was the type of actor gently described as an "old comedian." He had been born in England in the 1770s, was a brother-in-law of the well-known English actor Charles Kemble, and claimed to be a personal friend of George IV. He had come to America in 1823, had established a southern theatrical circuit and, before the end of the decade, would take up dairy farming in Texas and die.[6] In DeCamp's 1831 summer season, the height of Preston's achievement was his characterization of Antipholus of Ephesus in *A Comedy of Errors*. When the company toured to Quebec City, Preston was once again eclipsed by his wife, who "was tender as Tarquinia" in a production of *Brutus* starring Charles Kean.[7] The Montreal season, like many before, provided the couple with a means of survival but did nothing to further their careers.[8]

By 1835 the unquenchable Preston was once more in the southern states. The *Charleston Mercury* for March 5 and 6, 1834, lists Mrs Preston in the casts of *Douglas* and *The Soldier's Daughter*, and praised her highly: "Her talent is so well known and so universally appreciated, that any communication from us would be superfluous." The paper contains no mention of Preston himself. However, by the following year, he had definitely embarked on his career as actor-manager. Beginning a pattern which he would continue to follow for the next two decades, even though it brought him nothing more than transitory success, Preston announced to the public of Raleigh, North Carolina, that "having become the lessee of the principal Theatres in the State, viz. Raleigh, Wilmington, and Newbern [sic], he has just returned from the North, where he has succeeded in engaging, from the different Theatres, a strong and efficient *Corps Dramatique*, whose talents cannot be surpassed by any stock company in the United States."[9]

Preston's strategy was to bring drama to areas where theatrical competition did not exist. Unfortunately, lack of dramatic activity in any particular locale usually meant that the area's theatrical facility was in great need of repair, and thus the inexperienced manager was forced to commit his financial resources to the town carpenter before seeing any return on his investment. Following this pattern, he advertised to the public of Raleigh, in November 1835, that he had repaired the theatre which "of late years, [had been] so neglected as to render it almost unfit and uncomfortable for Ladies to enter."[10] Further, he successfully petitioned the theatre's owners to allow him two rent-free weeks as he not only had "gone to considerable expense in painting and repairing the front of said building," but found that he would also have to repaint and repair the scenery.[11] Despite his work on the building and his organization of the touring circuit, Preston's stay in North Carolina lasted less than two months, not long enough for him to recoup his investment.

Possibly he looked on his move from Raleigh to Charleston, South Carolina, early in 1836, not as a break from but as an expansion of his theatrical circuit. In any case, in late February the *Charleston Mercury* announced to its readers that Mr Preston "has at considerable expense fitted up a new theatre."[12] With Preston as manager and Mrs Preston as star, the New Theatre moved peacefully through its first two weeks. This new start, however, was shortlived. Scarcely a fortnight after the opening, the same newspaper announced that Talbot Watts had replaced Preston as proprietor of the New Theatre.[13] Two weeks after that takeover, Mr W.M. Lanning supplanted Watts, and "purchased the wardrobe formerly belonging to Mr Decamp [sic]."[14] Buoyed no doubt by this new finery, Preston remained as an actor in his former company until late April.

In September, Preston and his wife moved north to the Philadelphia stage where they had been hired by F.C. Wemyss. In his first week, Preston played Soloman and Mrs Preston played Mrs Haller opposite J.B. Booth's lead in *The Stranger*. On the following night (September 7), Preston played Polonius to Booth's Hamlet. J.B. Booth had surrendered to alcohol by this time, but he remained one of the greatest actors of his day.

Playing opposite such an actor, and doing so on the famous Walnut Street stage, was undoubtedly the highlight of the decade for Preston. Yet, despite such an auspicious opening at one of America's foremost theatres, Preston's career, anchored in mediocrity, did not take flight. Charles Durang, stage manager at the Walnut Street Theatre, was less than impressed by Preston's acting.

Mrs Preston was a small, thin woman, with black eyes and pretty, regular features. Her requisites for acting were all effective, but entirely founded on nature. She was not burdened with anything like cultivated mental qualities. Her voice was loud and sonorous, with little studied modulation. She always seemed to please, and was a favorite with the Walnut audience. In her private life she was of a retired nature, seemingly amiable. Her husband was a poor actor.[15]

Mrs Preston played lead roles throughout the fall season: Gertrude to Booth's Hamlet, Queen to his Richard III, Margaret to his Sir Giles in *A New Way to Pay Old Debts*, and Florinda to his Apostate. She played the title role in *The Maid of Cashmere* for a solid week, and began January 1837 playing the lead in *Black Eyed Susan*. But Preston, as Durang's sketch suggests, quickly sank into the middle ranks of Wemyss's company. By mid-November he had left his wife to finish the season before appreciative Philadelphia audiences and had returned to soldier on once more in the south.

Although he had already lost two theatres and one company in his six-month season in the Carolinas, Preston remained undaunted. The *North Carolina Standard* of November 10, 1836, announced to the good citizens of Raleigh that Preston had returned and was ready, once again, to "open the campaign." Preston's was one of the last two professional theatre companies to reside in Raleigh before the Civil War.[16] This time, tempering enthusiasm with experience, Preston made no announcements of long-term plans for a state-wide theatre circuit. Possibly, he looked upon the return to Raleigh as a respite which would give him the opportunity to plan his next move. In any case, his second Raleigh season opened in November and lasted scarcely a month.

By early December the *Richmond Whig and Public Advertiser* was announcing to the citizens of Virginia those same productions which, scant weeks earlier, Preston had offered in North Carolina. For the previous four years, Richmond had faced "acute theatrical depression."[17] Newspapers for 1832-1835 advertise a total of eight performances; in 1833, the playhouse stockholders had been unsuccessful in their attempt to unload the theatre; and there is no record of any theatrical activity in Richmond in the twelve months before Preston arrived.[18] The now-cautious Preston tested the Richmond waters with a short season beginning early in December and ending in February, 1837. Satisfied with the response, he closed the dilapidated theatre for two weeks in order to add new scenery and a drop curtain, and to "repair and clean" the House from floor to ceiling.[19] Mrs Preston, her Philadelphia season behind her, had briefly strengthened the company before accepting more lucrative employment elsewhere. The theatre reopened for a spring season, ran for two months, and then closed so abruptly that the company did not have time for their customary benefit performances. The hasty closing grew out of a dispute between the Irish comedian Tyrone Power and Preston, but one southern historian's blunt assessment of the season concluded that "the combination of poor management, poor company, poor theater, and hard times provided less than ideal conditions for a theatrical renaissance in Richmond."[20] More generally, across the south, forces of morality were mounting another offensive against the iniquity of the stage. For one with theatrical abilities as modest as Preston's, it was time to move on. His Richmond closing, on April 14, 1837, kept intact Preston's record for losing every southern theatre he renovated. With his third theatre lost, he closed his southern campaign, gathered a few members of his Richmond company, and headed north.

Two months after leaving Richmond, the peripatetic Preston opened for a summer season at the Theatre Royal in Montreal with what he termed "a strong and efficient company," but which the *Montreal Gazette* described as "small but select."[21] Beginning on a light note with the old chestnut *Honey Moon*, Preston's opening two weeks starred Mr Oxley, a youthful tragedian from Preston's Richmond company, who essayed Hamlet, Damon, and Virginius with more energy than maturity. Mrs Preston, who arrived in the middle of July, was judged "a finished and successful actress" by the Gazette for her performances in *The Wife of Mantua* and *Charles II*.[22] But even her star was diminished as, with the arrival of that shortlived but interesting theatrical phenomenon, Cony and Blanchard's dog dramas, she was forced to play second lead to Hector, a Newfoundland dog disguised as *The Grateful Lion*. It was a lackluster month both artistically and financially. The *Montreal Gazette*, following the productions closely, balanced gentle criticism of the company's other actors with harsh reproofs for the beleaguered stage manager, who seemed unable to attend to backstage duties while simultaneously treading the boards in support roles. Preston's own acting received praise: "We had thought that Mr. Preston's forte was comedy, and were agreeably disappointed on finding him act the character of Valerius [in *Brutus*] with much propriety and discretion."[23] Montreal's Theatre Royal had been built in 1825, and would be demolished in 1844. In its whole sorry history, no actor-manager was financially successful in the building.[24] The best that could be said for Preston's Montreal season is that, though it was plagued by profitless houses, the summer passed without incident. This lack of remarkable incident itself makes the Canadian season remarkable.

Despite his southern defeats, Preston remained firm in his belief that success was linked to the setting up of a prosperous theatrical circuit. A circuit would provide both a stable basé from which to mount a production and a wider population from which to draw a ticket-buying audience. The goal was to generate an audience equivalent in size to that possible in a large city without the risks inherent in depending on any one place. The Montreal experience showed that setting up in the wrong town at the wrong time made financial success difficult. Yet Preston's question was never whether theatre would ever be financially rewarding, but rather where to establish his next circuit.

Preston's last, and most successful, season before coming to eastern Canada was spent in Albany. The New York state capital seemed to offer precisely the conditions for which he was looking. The city had a tradition of theatre, but no resident company. As well, the theatre could draw from surrounding centres such as Troy, Schenectady and Waterford. And, further afield, there was potential for a touring circuit. Without first remodeling the theatre, manager Preston opened in Albany on September 17, 1838. It was a long ambitious season, supported almost nightly by Mrs Preston; during the first week alone the Albany public was offered *Rob Roy*, followed by J.B. Booth in *Richard III, Hamlet,* and *Othello*. The following week included

King Lear, Macbeth, A New Way to Pay Old Debts, and *The Hunchback*. In early October, Preston added the contemporary classics: *The Lady of Lyons, The Belle's Stratagem, Damon and Pythias, The Stranger, Brutus* and *Virginius*. In November, Edwin Forrest, the most popular and talented American tragedian of the period, offered his *Metamora* three times in the same week. In a sorry comment on the times and the tastes of the popular audience, Preston concluded his season at the end of November with the same dog dramas which had brought his Montreal season to a close the previous year. The *Albany Argus*'s exhortation to its readers to turn out for Preston's benefit on the final night sounded a familiar chord: "It has not, probably, been a profitable [season], but it has proved that Mr. Preston is determined to deserve success, if he cannot command it."[25].

As might be predicted, Preston decided that Albany's potential warranted renovation of the theatre. He kept his company busy by touring south to such centres as Hudson and Poughkeepsie while the repairs were made.[26] Just before Christmas, Preston made his by-now-familiar announcement that his theatre had "undergone every alteration and repair which exclusive study for . . . individual comfort and convenience could suggest."[27] Preston was also willing to trim his sails to the desires of his audience. Since the classics had not proved profitable, he was more than willing to mount more popular entertainments. Thus his second season, opening on Christmas Eve, 1838, rarely rose above the level of *The Olympic Devils, The Black Domino* and *Rose D'Amour*. Citing the need for even further repairs to the theatre, Preston suspended his winter season at the end of January, led his company to a "temporary building, fitted up for their reception" in Troy for three weeks, and then returned to Albany for one more month.[28] Near the end of March, word filtered down to Preston that the building's stockholders were so unhappy with their lack of profit that they had turned the building over to a religious organization. With the die cast, Preston offered the Albany audience a week of Shakespearean tragedy. Unfortunately, his taste was not shared by the populace. On his final night, the frustrated actor-manager offered his Albany audience *The Hypocrite* and a new piece called *H.W. Preston* or *The Manager in Distress*. In a farewell to the theatre and its manager, the *Albany Argus* wrote:

We must bear witness to the excellence of the stage arrangements during Mr. Preston's management. We have had the talent of the day—indeed, every inducement has been held out to make the Theatre worthy of patronage. That it has not succeeded equal to the merits of the gentleman, we know is in no degree owing to his want of activity.[29]

Preston attempted to continue his Albany venture by raising a subscription for a new theatre. But the response was less than adequate. The actor-manager, bereft of still another theatre, could only move on.

Less than two months after his eviction, Henry W. Preston opened in Saint John, New Brunswick. How or why he made the leap from upstate New York to the eastern coast of Canada is unknown, but the celerity with which the move was executed suggests either desperation or inspiration. The Saint John location offered to this most determined of actor-managers a sizable population base, a large area presently enjoying only passing exposure to professional theatre, and the option of setting up a circuit, by sea, of the principal centres of Nova Scotia and Newfoundland. Preston remained active in the Maritimes longer than in any other area. While there are gaps in the record of his travels, newspapers show that his first season in Saint John extended from May to September, that he then toured to Halifax, and returned to Saint John about six weeks later for another season. In 1840, he opened in Saint John in June, played there until September, and again toured to Halifax. He mounted his third season in Saint John in June, 1841, before moving on once more to Halifax in August. Although there is no record of where he spent the winters and springs of these three years, the consistency of this pattern suggests that Preston had finally achieved his theatrical ambition of setting up a successful touring circuit. Possibly, in order to escape the Canadian winters, he extended his tour southwards. Alternatively, Charlottetown newspapers hailed his 1844 arrival with a familiarity that suggests that he performed, sometime during this 1839-1841 period, on Prince Edward Island. Speculation aside, a playbill for the Halifax Theatre announced that, following the troupe's final performance, on October 19, 1841, Preston was opening a season in Newfoundland and that he would return to Halifax in six weeks.[30]

Preston's decision to tour to Newfoundland was injudicious. He already had a touring circuit which, for the previous three years, had provided him with his first sustained success. St. John's broke this pattern. His six weeks stretched into seven months, and even then a local editor described Preston's efforts as "very inadequately rewarded," and the actor-manager himself bluntly called them "profitless."[31] Preston disappeared from the St. John's papers in the summer of 1842. But the *St. John's Times* for April 26, 1843 (eighteen months after Preston's departure from Halifax) carries an advertisement for an evening of theatre involving Mrs Preston, a few remnants of the Halifax company, and the amateurs of the town. Preston was obviously either once again, or still, in Newfoundland. The inclusion of local amateurs in his productions suggests that the actor-manager and his company had fallen on very hard times—a fact underlined by an advertisement in the *Public Ledger* in which Thomas Preston, one of Henry Preston's troupe, offered his scene-painting talents to anyone needing "imitations of woods and marbles in a style superior to any seen by him in this country."[32]

In the fall of 1843, Preston sailed for the States in search of new strength for his Newfoundland company. Perhaps Mrs Preston accompanied him on the trip south. If so, he returned alone. In the years immediately before Preston began performing in eastern Canada, Mrs Preston had been working in New York.[33] She had left the New York stock companies and accompanied her husband to Canada in 1839, and she was with him on Newfoundland as late as the spring of 1843. But, around the time of Preston's trip south in the fall of 1843, while her husband's Newfoundland fortunes were at an extremely low ebb, her name began reappearing in the theatrical records of New York's Chatham and Bowery theatres. The Preston marriage was over. Nevertheless, the undaunted manager, with his company strengthened by at least one new actor, returned and opened a winter season in St. John's in 1843.[34]

Preston began his campaign on November 8, with a production of *Damon and Pythias* under the patronage of Sir John Harvey. In an opening address, Preston prayed for the financial backing which ever eluded his efforts:

> Friends of the drama, Guardians of its fame,
> Let not our humble efforts plead in vain,
> But let your favours our endeavours cheer.
> Welcome the *New-born* babe, the *drama here.*
> By cold neglect cross not the budding smile

> But bid fair genius flourish here awhile,
> Look kindly on and every bounty give—
> By crowded houses bid the *infant* live.[35]

Preston's opening success was quickly followed by *Hamlet, Richard III*, and Payne's *Brutus*. Two weeks into his season, earnest of future profits inspired the actor-manager to close for a week in order to carry out some renovations on the theatre. He reopened with productions of *School for Scandal, Macbeth, Othello, King Lear*, and *Richelieu*. In *Brutus*, Preston played Titus "to the life; indeed the scenes produced between him and his father Mr. Rodney, seemed more like reality than fiction."[36] *Brutus* had been good for Preston. Years earlier, in Montreal, his acting of Valerius in the same play had brought forth similar comment.

The crowded houses for which Preston had pleaded on opening night were not to be. The unevenness of audience response led him to abandon the British classics, and by Christmas he was offering musicals. In January, 1844, he sought success with such populist drama as *The Robber's Wife, The Swiss Peasant Girl*, and *The Idiot Witness*. But nothing worked. A letter to the editor of the *St. John's Times*, at the end of January, revealed that Preston had, once again, been more optimistic than judicious:

> Mr. Editor—I perceive . . . that Mr. Preston, who has been catering for our public amusement during the fall and winter, (but, I fear, poor Preston! with little profit to yourself) announces his name for a "benefit" on Friday next; and, it is hoped that not only his friends, but every lover of the Drama, will take into consideration his "arduous and uphill task" during the last three months, and give him at least *one good house* on Friday evening, to enable him to relieve himself from the heavy liabilities he has incurred.[37]

This was only wishful thinking. In February, one of his actresses, Miss Hildreth, was reduced to announcing her "farewell performance" even though she was not leaving.[38] In March, a company actor advertised a "Grand Concert" for the ladies and gentlemen of St. John's "in consequence of the depressed state of the Drama, which has placed various of its members in unpleasant circumstances."[39] The various members soldiered on until June when, this time truthfully, Miss Hildreth announced her "farewell benefit." Her announcement underlined the desperation of her situation: "it is hoped, that as the young lady is anxious to leave Newfoundland . . . the liberality of an ever-generous public will be extended in the present case of emergency."[40] Soon after, Preston, accompanied by two of his remaining company—notably Miss Hildreth, and the company musician Mr James—gave up the battle and sailed away from Newfoundland.

Perhaps Preston lacked the fare back to the United States or even to Nova Scotia. Certainly this would explain why he and his compatriots next found themselves on Prince Edward Island, a location close to the New Brunswick mainland but one with little potential for even a small professional company. An editorial in the *Islander* for August 16, 1844, announced that theatrical performances would be offered by Preston, "an old and tried caterer to the Dramatic taste of the Provincial Public on this side of the Straits," and expressed the hope (which Preston undoubtedly echoed) "that Charlottetown, limited though its resources may be, will evince a befitting appreciation of the Dramatic art, by the extension of a liberal and generous patronage to Mr. PRESTON." There is no record of the type of performance Preston had in mind for Charlottetown. His impecunious state would suggest that evenings of readings might stretch his financial resources to their limits. But this question soon became irrelevant when, as the *Islander* reported, a crowd of ruffians stoned the Masonic Lodge while Preston and Miss Hildreth were performing, breaking nearly every window in the building.[41] Two weeks later, the paper announced that "Miss Hildreth would respectfully inform the inhabitants of Charlottetown there will be a performance at the [Masonic Hall] this evening, for her Benefit, when she trusts she may not appeal to their generosity in vain."[42] Financially, Prince Edward Island was shaping up as another Newfoundland. It was time for Preston and his meagre troupe to move on.

The notice which Preston placed in the Fredericton *Headquarters* on December 11, 1844, and in Thomas Hill's *Loyalist* the following day passed over his company's recent trials and tribulations as if they had never occurred:

Mr Preston, Manager of the Provincial Theatres, in passing through Fredericton from Saint John, N.F. [sic] *via* Charlottetown, accompanied by several professional persons, would respectfully announce his intention of giving an Entertainment of Vocal and Instrumental Music, interspersed with DRAMATIC READINGS, from the most approved Authors . . . on which occasion, Mr James, the celebrated Violinist, and Miss Hildreth, well known as a vocalist and Actress, will perform a variety of English, Irish, and Scotch Melodies. Following this olio, readings from *Hamlet*, two compressed acts of *School for Scandal*, and the closing farce *The Day After the Wedding* were offered for the delectation of Fredericton's discerning public. Members of the troupe other than Miss Hildreth and Mr James are left unnamed in newspaper accounts of the season. But the group was obviously large enough to form at least the backbone of a performing company.

Receiving, no doubt, a kinder welcome than had been extended on either Newfoundland or Prince Edward Island, Preston seized the opportunity to escape further winter wandering by setting up a short Fredericton season. Combining his own remnants with the amateur players of the town, he was able to mount, over the next three weeks, a season which included such popular pieces as *The Stranger* and *Charles II*. Fredericton had never before seen such a wealth of theatre, and Thomas Hill's columns provided the indefatigable Preston with all the support his *Loyalist* could offer.

While scripts with British sympathies had led but to destruction the previous December in Newfoundland, the Fredericton audience responded positively to such fare. On New Year's Day, 1845, Preston presented *Douglas*, which Hill pronounced as "creditably sustained," to a full house.[43] He followed this by bringing forth from his theatrical bag of British favorites *Richard III*, *George Barnwell*, *Pizarro*, *Venice Preserved*, and *Jane Shore*. Again, the columns of the *Loyalist* praised Preston's ability. His Rolla, in *Pizarro*, "exceeded any of his former acting we had witnessed."[44]

Predictably, however, success turned Preston's attention to the hall in which his company of professionals and amateurs had been performing. He rented the Histrionic Association Hall, a "neat little theatre fitted up in Mr. March's building,"[45] for the duration of the Legislative session. He renovated it "after the style of the French and English theatres," and he grandly rechristened it the "New Olympic Theatre." Not only did he arrange for an orchestra and commission new scenery, he raised the stage and restructured the hall to include parquette, or orchestra, seating

expressly arranged for the reception of the gentry, the Members of Assembly, and strangers visiting Fredericton during the ensuing Session. Exclusive of, and quite apart from, the Parquette, will be erected a spacious Gallery, to accommodate 200 people, at half price, with two separate entrances, so as to prevent any intercourse with the Parquette and Gallery audiences.

Again, he welcomed his audience to his new venture with an appropriate address—a version of the speech recited most recently in Newfoundland. The sentiment remained the same; the words changed slightly:

> And let your smiles our first endeavours cheer—
> Welcome the new-born babe—the buskin here!
> By cold neglect crop not its budding smile,
> But bid fair Genius flourish here awhile![46]

The separate entrances leading in opposite directions suggest that Preston had at last found, albeit momentarily, the genteel acceptance of theatre for which he had long yearned. For such a clientele, he offered three plays a week "selected from the most approved authors with such care, as to merit approbation from the most fastidious."[47] Looking to the "most approved authors," and following after a season which had included playwrights such as Shakespeare, Sheridan and Otway, Preston opened his new season at the end of January, 1845, with a minor Irish comedy by Cherry, *The Soldier's Daughter*, and followed that slight offering with the heavily shop-worn *Honey Moon* of Tobin. The "most approved authors" for a Fredericton winter were obviously not the giants of theatre. Preston tried to balance his season with *Hamlet*, but the necessity of mounting such a demanding script with little rehearsal time and only three professional actors supported by the Fredericton Amateurs must have taken a toll on production values. Nevertheless, for his efforts Preston received encouragement both from Thomas Hill's columns and from a letter to the *Loyalist* editor that praised his "chaste theatrical representations."[48] For a while, it must have seemed to Preston that the gods were finally smiling.

The enthusiasm with which Hill reported on Preston's productions, coupled with the advance notice that Hill was able to give his readers concerning Preston's plans, leaves no doubt that, during the cold Fredericton winter, each man had discovered in the other a sympathetic spirit. This relationship led to an announcement in Hill's columns, directed at those

40

"who desire to spend an evening in the enjoyment of rational amusement," of a "new *Local Comedy* . . . called 'The Provincial Association, or, taxing one another.'"[49] Modestly, Hill chose not to mention that he himself was the author of Preston's new script. The opening night for this new "local comedy" was first announced for February 21. A measure of Preston's faith in the drawing power of Hill's *Provincial Association* can be seen in the actor-manager's decision to use this occasion for his own benefit performance. A measure of the production's shakiness can be seen in the fact that the premiere had to be postponed for four days. The production obviously needed more rehearsal time than Preston—or his creditors—could afford. Unfortunately for the budding playwright, the extra four days were still insufficient to bring Hill's script to acceptable production standards. The opening night performance, on Tuesday, February 25, was less than stellar.

In his paper two days later, Hill tried to put the best face on the opening night. He reported that the first two acts had been "well sustained," but that the scenes which followed "were too intricate to be well performed on a first representation."[50] As well, there had been "some confusion" with the scenery, and "one or two of the Amateurs [had been] deficient in their parts." On a more positive note, Hill believed that "Miss Hildreth played the Tailor's wife to perfection." He closed his review with the anguished plea of a playwright who had just seen his first script mangled:

> Those who witnessed the performance on Tuesday night we would advise to go again, as it was impossible to judge of the merits of the piece from that representation; and we are assured that Mr. Preston has taken such precautions that they will not again be disappointed.

The other Fredericton papers, out of either diffidence or reluctance to offer free publicity to anything written by their competitor, ignored the script entirely. Despite the problems of opening night, Preston had sufficent confidence to mount the production for a second time two days later, and Miss Hildreth was willing to use this second performance as her own benefit. But the play was not successful enough to rescue Preston from the financial catastrophe brought on by his overly-ambitious renovations. Despite Hill's free publicity, Preston was unable to satisfy his creditors. Only one week after the second

41

performance of *The Provincial Association*, Preston received a tip that the bailiff was about to pounce. Under cover of night, he fled downriver to Saint John.

Notes

1. H.P. Phelps, *Players of a Century* (1880; reprinted New York: Blom, 1972), 281.
2. F.C. Wemyss, *Chronology of the American Stage* (1866; reprinted New York: Blom, 1968), 105.
3. Quoted in John Cargill, *50 British Plays 1660-1900* (London: Pan Books, 1979), 208.
4. *Carolina Observer*, April 29, 1830; quoted by Donald J. Rulfs, "The Ante-bellum Professional Theater in Fayetteville," *North Carolina Historical Review* 31 (April 1954), 128.
5. *Montreal Gazette*, August 6, October 8, 1831.
6. William Carson, *The Theatre on the Frontier* (Chicago: University of Chicago Press, 1932), 172f.
7. *Montreal Gazette*, October 8, 1831.
8. Following this engagement, the couple probably turned south once more. T. Allston Brown's *History of the New York Stage* (1903; reprinted New York: Blom, 1968) lists them as members of the Richmond Hill Theatre company in 1833; but Joseph N. Ireland's *Records of the New York Stage* (1866-67; reprinted New York: Burt Franklin, 1968) describes the identical season as taking place in 1836 (Brown, I, 235; Ireland, II, 173). Either year could be correct, but Preston's theatrical activity throughout the south in the mid-1830s suggests that the couple might more conveniently have spent a season in New York in 1833. The paucity of information concerning these years suggests that the Prestons enjoyed little success.
9. Quoted by Donald J. Rulfs, "The Ante-bellum Professional Theater in Raleigh," *North Carolina Historical Review* 29 (July 1952), 352.
10. *Raleigh Register*, November 9, 1835.
11. Rulfs, "The Ante-bellum Professional Theater in Raleigh," 346.
12. *Charleston Mercury*, February 29, 1836.
13. *Charleston Mercury*, March 16, 1836.
14. *Charleston Mercury*, March 28, 1836.
15. Charles Durang, *A History of the Philadelphia Stage between the Years 1749 and 1855*, 3rd Series, chapter 48, 137. Published in the *Sunday Despatch*, Philadelphia, 1854-1960.

16. James H. Dormon, *Theatre in the Ante-bellum South* (Chapel Hill: University of North Carolina Press, 1967), 150.
17. Dormon, 145.
18. Dormon, 145.
19. *Richmond Whig,* February 17, 1837.
20. Dormon, 146.
21. *Gazette,* June 17, 24, 1837.
22. *Gazette,* July 11, 1837.
23. *Gazette,* July 11, 1837. The season ran from June 26 to July 25, 1837.
24. Y.S. Bains, "Popular-Priced Stock Companies and Their Repertory in Montreal and Toronto in the 1890s," *Canadian Drama* 12 (1986), 332.
25. *Argus,* November 26, 1838.
26. Phelps, 215.
27. *Albany Journal,* December 21, 1838.
28. Phelps, 215.
29. *Argus,* March 30, 1839.
30. Performance calendar information for Saint John can be found in Mary Elizabeth Smith's *The Maritime Stage No 1: Saint John, 1789-1899* (Saint John: Division of Humanities and Languages, UNBSJ, 1987). The Halifax Theatre playbill is found in the Harvard Theatre Collection.
31. *Public Ledger,* June 21, 1842.
32. *Public Ledger,* July 4, 1843.
33. George C. D. Odell, *Annals of the New York Stage* (New York: Columbia University, 1927-1949), IV, 157.
34. *St. John's Times,* October 25, 1843.
35. *Public Ledger,* November 10, 1843. This is a section from a much longer address.
36. *Public Ledger,* November 21, 1843.
37. *St. John's Times,* January 24, 1844.
38. *St. John's Times,* February 7, 1844.
39. *St. John's Times,* March 6, 1844.
40. *St. John's Times,* June 5, 1844.
41. *Islander,* August 23, 1844.
42. *Islander,* September 6, 1844.
43. *Loyalist,* January 2, 1845.
44. *Loyalist,* January 16, 1845.
45. *Head Quarters,* January 1, 1845.
46. *Loyalist,* January 9, 1845.
47. *Head Quarters,* January 29, 1845.

48. *Loyalist,* February 17, 1845.
49. *Loyalist,* February 8, 1845.
50. *Loyalist,* February 27, 1845.

Chapter Three

A Pindaric Ode

"He counted them at close of day"
"And when the sun rose, *where* were they?"
                                                    BYRON

Twin sisters of the immortal nine,
By early Greece esteem'd the most divine,
        Thalia and Melpomene,
You who originally taught the art
Of acting *moving* dramas in a Cart,
(Which Classic Custom by the bye, to me
Serves to account for Justices hard-hearted
Believing still that Strollers should be carted)
Attune old Pindar's rusty Lyre again,
And for the theme's sake—oh! inspire the strain.
From Prester John is Pr-st-n's high descent,
The Great Mogul an arbitrary gent,
        Too partial to the sack and dirk,
"The Manager," so Williams oft allowed,
As for unpaid arrears he humbly bowed
        "*Was a great Turk.*"

When Prince Aeneas saw his palace burn,
And Troy devoted Troy! to tinder turn,
        He left his wife behind and took to sea.
        Thus Preston—you the Bowery left behind
And with a valiant steadfastness of mind
Led to new *scenes* the hungry company,
Resolved in mimic fields of fight to die
Feigned death secures him life's reality.

As when the Shepherd on the mountains height,
Beholds at once, with awe and pleasure too,

45

A long tailed Comet dart its fiery light,
Along the shining fields of starlit blue.
So gazed the good folks of our peaceful Town,
    When the OLYMPIC rose to view.

"Rose like an exhalation" some did frown
And said "*it did not promise much*" a lie,
Which the long play bills pasted up and down,
Plainly disproved to every seeing eye.
For there in pink and yellow blue and green,
Most *flam*-ing protestations might be seen,
Where the last work was still *variety*,
Others again the youthful and the vain,
Who thought with Bottom they could do the Lion,
And roar so "gently"—boldly would maintain
Of true civilization twas a scion.
That would do honour to the parent tree,
And for *their* parts—*they* would go the plays to see.

But there was one amongst the latter class
His pockets fill'd with gold—his heart with pride,
Who held that every poor man was an ass,
Ergo—possessed of no small share of chink,
    He scrupled not to think.
Himself as wise a man as ever lived and died,
    He chuckled inwardly to see
This Preston's growing popularity.
Reckoning on having rare additions made,
    If the tide held
And this Theatric passion swelled,
To his, already, heavy stock in trade,
But Fortune angry now to see the clown
She had enriched despise her, with a frown,
Kicked round her wheel—dispell'd self-approbation,
And dished for once our Solon's speculation,
Now Mercury looked down from his abode,
In a small lodge—on heaven's turnpike road
And saw his votary Preston's neat *Parquette*,
Crammed full of baliffs—by our Dives set,
To nab the Thespian for debt.
Enraged he sent a wily sprite
To the Hotel beneath the cloud of night,

And bid him deep implant in Preston's heart
The inclination for a start.

The Bills are out once more
    Larger and Larger,
These words on every door,
    "The company's much stronger."
"Gentlemen Amateurs have thought it fit
To patronize the Preston benefit!!"
With much more of the same verbosity
To stimulate the public curiosity.
But here the Muse must in heroics flow
As trumpeters, ere closing, loudest blow.
When friendly Night her sable veil let fall
And Somnus in his mantle shaded all,
The cautious Preston with his hardy crew
To Fredericton for ever bade adieu.
No boastful drums were beat upon the way
No spangled banners wooed the winds to play—
With prudent haste he bravely led the van
Behind the Chieftain came his faithful clan.
Nor stayed the march until their eager eyes,
Beheld the sheltering City's turrets rise,
Enough our Pegasus, the goal at last
Hast gained; a smile repays each labour past.

JUVENIS JOCOSUS[1]

1845 started off auspiciously for Preston. The winter season in Fredericton had brought with it a degree of success immeasurably beyond his recent experience. True, "the Chief," as he was known to his friends, had lost both his theatre and his audience. But, after the slings and arrows of Newfoundland and Prince Edward Island, he doubtlessly accepted such a situation with a fair degree of equanimity. The momentum he had achieved in Fredericton had been disrupted temporarily, but his entire career had been shaped by such uncontrollable events. On a more positive note, the lucky tip concerning the bailiff's imminent arrival had given the resilient manager time to pack his theatrical paraphernalia before taking flight to Saint John. Also, he had gained the friendship of Thomas Hill—whose script he carried with him in his retreat from Fredericton. And, for the first time, his leaving of a town had been immortalized by some pseudonymous bard.

Miss Hildreth's Fredericton benefit performance of *The Provincial Association* took place on February 27. On March 7, according to the Saint John *Courier*, Preston, "with a select company of Theatricals," opened in the port city with a production of the script which had delighted his Fredericton audience on various occasions the preceding December, Kotzebue's *The Stranger*.[2] The lack of free publicity, or "puffs," in the Saint John papers for the next months is most likely linked to Preston's failure to take out paid advertisements in those papers. This failure suggests that "the Chief" had not left his financial problems behind him when he had slipped away from the Fredericton bailiff. The celerity with which Preston had made his Fredericton exodus and opened in Saint John suggests that he did not have time to gather around himself a new company of professionals. Thus, the "select" company touted in the *Courier* was undoubtedly the same troupe that had loyally followed him down river. It was a company whose individual members, other than Preston and Miss Hildreth, Hill's *Loyalist* columns had rarely considered worthy of individual mention. With an empty purse and undistinguished actors, Preston recognized the necessity for radical—but economical—action.

No one could be more haunted by the spectre of failure than Preston. His theatrical ventures, stretching from Montreal to Raleigh and Richmond, had never succeeded. Within the past year alone, his Newfoundland company had broken up, his performance had been stoned on Prince Edward Island, and he had lost his newly renovated theatre in Fredericton. Lack of audience response to his new season in Saint John had quickly forced him to lower his ticket prices. He desperately needed a hit. And so he turned to Hill's *Provincial Association*. Because Preston had last left Saint John in 1841, around the time that Hill had arrived, the actor-manager might not have appreciated the depth of political animosity Hill's personality and writings had roused. Furthermore, Preston's Newfoundland ordeal had also occurred at the same time as Hill's editorial battle over the aims of the group calling itself the Provincial Association. And Preston certainly did not know that some of the play's characters were modelled after well-known Saint John businessmen. The script which had played so peaceably in Fredericton would, from Preston's perspective, allow a local issue to be explored before the very audience for whom it was relevant. He could not pass up this chance for success.

It is difficult to believe that Preston's friend Hill would not have known how the victims of his satire would receive the play. Hill's one previous venture into drama, which had taken place on the theatrical boards of Saint John a few years earlier, had taught him the danger of live theatre:

> We never supposed that we possessed the powers of a Garrick or a Kemble, but we were once advised—perhaps ill advised—to take part with the St. John Amateurs. It happened that most of the occupants of the Gallery on that evening were our personal or political enemies, and *the moment we appeared on the stage* we were hissed. We were not hissed off, however . . . but went through the part.[3]

The Provincial Association gave Hill the opportunity both to retaliate for this theatrical ambush and to add to his burgeoning collection of enemies by satirizing an organization that included many influential Saint Johners. The Provincial Association, a powerful group of merchants recently formed to lobby for provincial protective tariffs, considered Hill a turncoat because he first supported their ideals and then condemned them personally in his editorial columns as individuals whose concerns were "no more nor less than to benefit themselves by gulling the community."[4] Branded thereafter as a traitor to the merchants' cause, the playwright had nothing to lose by subjecting their organization to public ridicule. The unanswered question is this: did Hill allow his friend to innocently enter this lion's den, or did an informed Preston speculate that this violently controversial script might provide his box office with a fiscal windfall?

Preston's first performance of *The Provincial Association* in Saint John passed without incident at the end of March, 1845. But, according to Fenety's *Morning News*, it engendered "angry feelings" which the Saint John mayor should have recognized as a prelude to danger.[5] Preston, possibly mindful of such feelings but certainly aware of the financial potential of his production, quickly scheduled a second performance for April 2nd. The interim between the two performances provided Hill's enemies with the time needed to plan their attack.

The Saint John newspapers chronicle the results of Preston's impetuousness. Because such accounts do not point out the strong animosity felt against Hill by at least a segment of the Saint John public, and neglect to mention the rancour which existed between Hill and the other journalists, and fail to acknowledge any awareness of Preston's possibly non-artistic motives for mounting such a production, these evaluations of the uproar illustrate the pitfalls of accepting newspaper narratives as unbiased fact. The *fact* was that supporters of the group calling itself the Provincial Association had stationed themselves both inside and outside Preston's theatre, and had agreed upon the opening curtain of the second performance as their cue to riot. Those inside opened the door for their ticketless cohorts, and, in the grand tradition, the mob vented its anger over the script by attempting to demolish the building. The *significance* of this action depends on whose interpretation of it one accepts.

The editor of the Saint John *Herald* took the road of moral indignation against the rioters:

> On Wednesday evening last, this place of public amusement was a scene of uproar and confusion, which reflects the deepest disgrace on the parties who composed the mob. It appears that a gang of reckless and unthinking persons took offence at the new play which was announced for performance on that evening, and were predetermined to suppress it at all hazards. This they effected—for so violent was the tumult in the theatre and in the street that it was impossible for the performers to get a hearing.

Clearly, from the viewpoint of the *Herald*, the problem was not in the play but rather in the minds and actions of the rioters:

> The unmerited prejudice against the play originated in absolute ignorance of its meaning. The silly supposition that Mr. Preston or any other Manager, would produce on the boards of his theatre, a piece that would hurt the feelings of the public, is too ridiculous to be entertained by any one. Those who are in the habit of catering for the Public patronage are actuated by motives of an opposite description; and ignorant indeed must that man be who supposes for a moment that the Play of the "Provincial Association" is anything more than a sportive delineation of the incident upon which it is founded.[6]

Such a defense presumes that Preston or Hill would act only from totally rational motives. It fails to take into consideration either the playwright's proclivity for stirring whatever pot might

50

be boiling at the time or the manager's desperate financial situation. Also, the *Herald*'s defense might have been more selfish than naive—that newspaper's office was selling tickets to the production. According to George Fenety in his *Morning News*, the *Herald*'s editor was being guided solely by monetary considerations and did not care "whether he fell from the dignity of his profession, and turned himself into a vender of Theatrical tickets or not, so long as it was in the cause of pounds, shillings, and pence and he could realize 'something worth while' by the prostitution."[7] Evaluation of the *Herald*'s moral censure of the mob is made more complex because whether or not the newspaper made money on the production has nothing to do with whether the rioters were justified or merely barbarous.

While Fenety was quick to point out the mote of hypocrisy in the *Herald*'s account, he missed the double-edged beam in his own. Fenety viewed theatre in general as a nuisance to be suffered but avoided. More to the point, his viciously personal editorial war with this particular playwright had been going on ever since Hill took over the editorial chair of the *Loyalist*. In any case, while the *Herald* had placed the blame for the riot entirely at the feet of the rioters, the *Morning News* placed responsibility with Hill, Preston, and even the city's mayor:

> It is very seldom that we condescend to notice this sink of iniquity [the Theatre]; and we only do it now, in order to bring out some facts, connected with Wednesday evening's performances—and so remind the Manager of the Theatre of his audacity, for coming before the public, to libel certain members of the community, on account of certain principles which they profess to uphold. His Worship the Mayor, has likewise much to answer for in the present case. . . .[8]

Having thus dismissed the concept of theatre generally, Fenety proceeded to confess astonishment that Preston "should come to St. John with such contamination in his pocket; and then expect countenance and support from a British community, who know as well how to resent an insult, as the people of which he is an off-shoot; a people who have more than once driven a British actor from their boards, for offences too insignificant to be compared for a moment, with the one which he himself has just now been guilty of." While Preston was accountable for producing the play, the mayor was to be condemned for allowing it to go on. It had already been performed once, so the mayor, from Fenety's perspective, should have known that the satire was bound to provoke "angry feelings."

In apportioning the blame, it would have been too much to expect that Fenety would allow the playwright to escape uncensured. The mayor was simply apathetic. Preston and his actors were merely "mouthpieces." But the author, "a miserable wretch, only remarkable for his scurrility," was nothing more than a "worthless fellow" of whom "nothing better could be expected." Underlining his point, Fenety went on to call Hill "a mercenary dog [who] could be hired to do any thing—for a shilling he would hang his mother." The rioters, on the other hand, were on the side of virtue. They had attended "a libellous performance . . . for the purpose of putting it down, and driving every actor from the stable into the street, as they would a wolf, who has become a common nuisance to them."

The actual events of the riot have been passed down in vivid detail by Fenety who, in line with his beliefs, did not himself attend the "sink of iniquity":

As far as we can learn (of course we were not present ourselves) the Theatre was crowded; while outside there were upwards of three hundred persons, all ready for a row. The *Farce* was played first; and it passed off without molestation. After some other *trumpery* was got through with, the grand piece of the evening, called "The Provincial Association," was brought on by the *troupe*; and this was the challenge to arouse the angry passions of the multitude. War was immediately declared after the sounding of the *tocsin*; then all Bedlam broke loose—the first attack was upon the stove-pipe; this was demolished in a twinkle, while the hissing, yelling, hooting, whistling and stamping, we are told, was awfully terrific.

The crowd outside took up the response, the doors were forced open,and the rabble entered 'upon the free ticket,' and took possession of the citadel; some of them were armed with clubs, sticks, and other implements . . . the work of destruction was going on among the benches and other appointments at a fearful rate.

Editor Fenety went on to describe the ineffectuality of the mayor's appearance, the incompetence of the police, and the crassness of the play's defenders. He ended with the disgruntled observation that "this is the second row in St. John within a few weeks; and this might have been prevented without any difficulty, had proper steps been taken for that end."

The editors quickly moved on from the attack on the Theatre to the attacks they had made on each other. George Fenety had already called the *Herald* editor a prostitute. The *Herald* pointed out that George Fenety's remarks "were perfectly worthy of their author; that is to say, extremely good-natured, and egregiously untrue—untrue as respects many things 'recorded' by him, and flagrantly abusive of individuals too far above his contemptible malignity."[9] And Thomas Hill, observing from both the physical and the editorial distance of Fredericton, reinforced the *Herald*'s attack on Fenety:

> The lick-trencher Publisher of the News, ever ready to pander to the worst vices of the community, if by so doing he supposes he can sell an extra number of his *penny trumpets*, comes out with a flaming editorial, in which he grossly misrepresents the play, of which he proves himself to be entirely ignorant, applies to us the most scurrilous epithets as the author of the play, abuses Preston for presuming to bring such a *libellous* production in his pocket from Fredericton, abuses the mayor . . . grossly misrepresents the riots . . . encourages the rioters . . . and *falsely* charges a very respectable mercantile gentleman of Portland with having led a party of his men to the Theatre to support the performers! Could baseness, ignorance, insolence and folly any further go?[10]

In his own defence, Hill claimed that he had written the play to provide Preston with a local script, and to provide "a little innocent amusement" to his audience. He denied that his characters were caricatures of Saint Johners, but confessed to wondering whether or not a farce based on the events surrounding the production might not be in order—with Fenety as one of the principal characters.

These motives surrounding the first Saint John theatre riot had shaped the accounts of the event for future generations almost as much as had the physical act itself. To Preston, what happened was that he had put on a play to which a certain faction objected, organized themselves, and badly damaged his theatre. It was an action to be defined in legal, rather than moral, terms. To the *Herald*, what happened was that a "gang of reckless and unthinking persons" who really did not understand what the play was about used this occasion for wanton misconduct—an anti-social action for which they would later feel deep personal embarrassment. To the *Morning News*, what happened that night was that moral and respectible citizens identified an insulting and libellous performance in their midst and extirpated it. And for Hill, the whole event was a misconstruction of an innocent script by personal and political enemies who were perfectly capable of intentionally misinterpreting anything he wrote. The truth of the matter depends on the angle from which it is viewed.

After the riot, Preston's Theatre was quickly reopened, and on the following Monday, April 7, *The Provincial Association* was once again placed before the citizens of Saint John. Fenety has favoured posterity with an epic account of Preston's attempt to mount his third performance of the play. After much negotiation between Preston, the mayor and the deputy sheriff, a plan emerged. The production was scheduled for one o'clock in the afternoon—a move calculated to force any rioters to pursue their wicked designs in broad daylight. As well, in an effort to keep out the riff-raff, Preston, guided no doubt by the purest motives any actor-manager faced with a potential sell-out audience could have, took the noble course of doubling his ticket prices. As a final precaution, tickets were sold only to persons willing to sign a requisition stipulating that they were particularly desirous of having this performance take place. Under these circumstances, according to Hill's account of the afternoon, the piece was performed "before a respectable audience, and went off without any riot . . . and some of the *prompters* of the riot being present, seeing the play, for the first time, *performed*, are said to be heartily ashamed of the course they have hitherto pursued."[11]

There is no reason to doubt that the performance went smoothly, once it got under way, and possibly the moral reform at which Hill hints did take place in the hearts of some of the riot's instigators. But what Hill ignored and Fenety found particularly ironic in the mass of troubles surrounding this performance was the relationship between Preston and the character he portrayed. Apparently, the play ends with the principal characters (one of whom was acted by Preston) being carted off to prison. Preston, having last left Saint John with his bills unpaid, had felt the threat of a similar fate. In a conflux of Art and Nature that Fenety found most satisfying, as Preston first entered the stage from the wings, one Officer Busteed mounted that same platform, seized Preston, and carted the unfortunate actor himself off to prison. When the significance of Preston's sudden removal from the theatre sank in, the audience was nonplussed. All the efforts and negotiations involved in remounting the play seemed to have come to naught. In Fenety's words:

It was a trying moment; and what was to be done under the circumstances? Finally it was concluded, rather than be made April fools of, after getting along so far, and so well—that poor Preston should be liberated from *durance vile*, by some of the company going bail for him. This was accordingly done, and the Chief was liberated, and came forward and performed his part to the edification of the audience.[12]

The lesson of the occasion was not lost on Preston. After this performance, the actor-manager allowed Hill's play to begin its quiet slide into obscurity. The events of the week did nothing to build theatrical crowds for the rest of the season, and Preston was left with only the memory of the day his tickets sold for 5s. But he was also saddled with an acting company of no particular talent, a theatre of no particular merit, and little money with which to advertise his remaining shows. The one paid advertisement that found its way into the *Courier*'s columns reflects how low the company had sunk. On the Monday following his arrest, Preston offered to Saint John's discerning public a performance of Coleman's *The Heir-at-Law*, in which the part of Dr. Pangloss was performed by a talented eleven year old boy.

Preston's immediate goal was survival, and his immediate problems included the quality of his facilities and the calibre of his actors. Other than the acting abilities of the long-suffering Miss Hildreth and himself, Preston had little with which to work. At the end of June, he opened a new theatre, The Prince of Wales', on the corner of Duke and Sydney streets. The impression he conveyed in his opening announcements was that he had designed and built the structure as a real theatre. But later accounts suggest that the building had formerly been a place of worship, known as the Tabernacle, run by a Mr Ambler. Having provided himself with a more suitable venue, Preston turned to the vexing problem of upgrading his troupe.

His first addition was Miss McBride, a actress from the American theatres. On paper, she must have appeared to be exactly what Preston needed. She was, presumably, the nine year old "Miss McBride" who played at New York's Pavilion

Theatre in 1818. She had begun her adult career at Boston's Federal Street Theatre on September 16, 1825 as Kate Hardcastle in Goldsmith's *She Stoops to Conquer*,[13] spent a decade in the acting company of Boston's Tremont Theatre (where she had played a small role in Miss Hildreth's Boston *debut* in 1838), made her New York *debut* at the prestigious and venerable Park Theatre opposite Ellen Tree in 1838,[14] and returned to the Tremont in 1842. In 1843, she spent a season with Wemyss's company at the Chestnut Street Theatre in Philadelphia. Just before coming to Saint John, she had returned to the Park where she acted with Macready and Booth. In spite of all this, however, her career had actually had few highlights. In the decade at the Tremont, she had never risen above minor roles and occasional solos as a *danseuse*; at the Park, she had been "wholly incapable" of filling the roles she had been given;[15] and, while she had indeed shared the stage with Macready and Booth, she had merely played small company roles in productions in which they had starred.

Even such a background was more than sufficient for Preston's needs. Miss McBride opened as Pauline, in *The Lady of Lyons*, at the end of June. Two days later, on July 2, she and Preston took the leads in *The Stranger*, and she ended her first week in *The Soldier's Daughter*. Over the next few weeks, her light shone forth in such feminine staples of the mid-nineteenth century stage as *The Wife* and *Lucelle*. Her radiance, however, was short-lived. When Preston's new male lead, a tragedian from the London stage who had starred in Preston's Saint John season of 1839, joined the company, the manager immediately shifted his repertoire to plays with strong masculine roles. The deposed Miss McBride spent most of August playing second leads in heroic dramas.

The public response to Miss McBride was mixed. One letter to the *Chronicle* pronounced her an actress whose talents would fit her for any theatre,[16] and she excited even George Fenety to confess that "we did not know which to admire most, the exhibition which she made in the tights, or her clever *naiveté* when ambling with her lover."[17] Possibly because she had lost the repertoire of leading roles she had enjoyed throughout July, she fell out with Preston, and one day, early in September, she refused to go on stage. In a letter to the *Chronicle*, Preston described her as an actress whose actions were "unjust, ungrateful, and unbecoming."[18] Miss McBride left

56

the company and Saint John, returned to New York, and there died of consumption the following year. But Preston was not unduly concerned with the departure of his female star, because the cause of her troubles, his new tragedian, was proving very popular. The Saint John audience seemed oblivious to the ineptitude of the rest of his company as long as Preston produced, at centre stage, the "Kean of the East End," Charles Freer.

Notes

1. *New Brunswick Reporter,* March 21, 1845.
2. *Courier,* March 8, 1845.
3. *Loyalist,* December 5, 1844.
4. *Loyalist,* April 10,1845.
5. *Morning News,* April 4, 1845.
6. *Herald,* April 4, 1845.
7. *Morning News,* April 9, 1845.
8. *Morning News,* April 4, 1845.
9. *Herald,* April 11, 1845.
10. *Loyalist,* April 10, 1845.
11. *Loyalist,* April 10, 1845.
12. *Morning News,* April 9, 1845.
13. William Clapp, *A Record of the Boston Stage* (1853; reprinted New York: Blom, 1968), 226.
14. Odell, IV, 207.
15. Odell, IV, 442.
16. *Chronicle,* September 5, 1845.
17. *Morning News,* September 8, 1845.
18. *Chronicle,* September 12, 1845.

Mr FREER as ALONZO the BRAVE in Alonzo

Chapter Four

The English actor Charles Freer first came to North America in 1839, lured by the same Siren call that had beckoned Preston and his more famous theatrical colleagues, luminous thespians whose names flowed trippingly from George Fenety's pen despite that editor's avowed distaste for the Dramatic Arts. Their objective was, naturally enough, not Art, but Money. Their catalyst had been Stephen Price, a theatrical entrepreneur active on both sides of the Atlantic who was "the equal of Charles Frohman in the scope of his enterprises and of Phineas Taylor Barnum in his flair for publicity."[1] Price began his career at New York's famous Park Theatre in 1808, and in 1810 he and his fellow lessee at the Park, T.A. Cooper, began importing English stars with the tour of George Frederick Cooke. Cooke had reached his peak at Covent Garden around the turn of the century. When he first appeared at the Park Theatre, "he completely eclipsed all who had been seen before him in this country."[2] Unfortunately, his theatrical successes had always been balanced by his alcoholic excesses. In spite of "the overriding triumph of his short sojourn" in America, he "was ill [with dropsy] and was destroying himself with drink;"[3] the "poisoned liquid completely unfitted him for his duties, and ultimately brought him to the grave."[4] Even so, his American box office receipts showed that the new world could indeed be a golden land for English actors.[5] Ten years later Price offered to his American audience Edmund Kean, a man "with the genius to have been more than a Garrick in his art [but also] the follies and passions at times to reduce him almost beneath a Cooke in his habits."[6] Kean saw in America not only its financial potential, but also a chance to bask in new adulation, to put the emotional effects of two recent paternity suits behind him, and to flee the affections of his demanding mistress, Charlotte Cox. His American tour began in November, 1820; by spring, he was sending £1000 a month to his English bankers and boasting in a letter that he was "making money and fame by bushels."[7] Kean's second tour, five years later, was less successful financially, but his abilities sustained his reputation as "the greatest of tragedians."[8]

In 1826, Stephen Price moved from New York's Park Theatre to London's Drury Lane following manager Ellison's bankruptcy there. With his new access to English actors, Price was able to supply American theatres, especially the Park, in which he retained an interest, with the much-sought English stars. Charles Macready began his first tour by packing the Park Theatre even before Edmund Kean's second American tour had ended. Macready's second tour, in 1843, was even more successful, and his final tour, which began in 1848, ended in one of the most famous evenings of the American theatre, the Astor Place riot. Compounding the success of the star system were J.B. Booth's two tours, in 1821 and 1824; Charles Kean's four tours, in 1830, 1839, 1845 and 1865; and the many tours by lesser stars of the British dramatic firmament. By the time Preston set sail for America, it had definitely become a land of theatrical promise. By the time of Freer's arrival, a decade later, the image of America as some sort of theatrical Nirvana was firmly planted in the minds of British actors and actresses.

In contrast to the handful who actually achieved fame and fortune on the American stage was the much larger group of English actors whose vision of prosperity in America came to grief against the hard realities of the star system. In order for the few to star, the many were forced to eke out their livelihoods in support. Allston Brown's chatty *History of the New York Stage* is littered with examples of theatrical unfortunates, English and American, who either took it upon themselves to end their miserable lives, or who were guided to their ends by an unkind Fate. The body of the insane John Winans, step-father to the young Dennin sisters who acted in Preston's 1845 company in Saint John and Fredericton, was found in a decomposed state with its flesh "almost off the bones." The unfortunate William S. Deverna, lessee of New York's Chatham Theatre, slipped from a balcony box late one evening, struck a chandelier, and fell to the stage where "he lay with a broken spine until death relieved him." Brown reserves his most melodramatic prose for the death of William Osborne, an English actor who had come to America to make his fortune; who had played supporting roles to Edmund Kean, Macready and Thomas Hamblin; and who, some years before his death, had "been lost sight of to the profession":

In a small, squalid room about ten feet square, on the top story of No. 5 Centre Market Place, between Grand and Broome Streets, the remains of the old actor, William E. Osborne, the friend of Forrest, the elder Wallack, and of Manager Simpson of the old Park Theatre, were laid out without a shroud or coffin to cover them. Two of his sons, pale, careworn young men, and their wives, sat in the room on rickety chairs, which, along with a stove, mahogany bureau, a cheap pine table, and a child's cradle, constituted all of the furniture of the chamber. A poor, pale-faced baby occupied the crib, and a hungry-looking boy of six years watched with eager eyes a pot boiling on the stove, with a broken plate for a cover. The corpse of the dead actor lay on the floor, under the shelf of the window, with an old counterpane thrown over it, and no preparations of any kind appeared to have been made for its decent removal and interment. . . .[9]

Between the celebrated tours of Booth, Macready and the Keans, on the one hand, and the melancholy ends endured by the actors for whom the path of American Theatre led but to the grave, fall the more substantial contributions of a third group of theatrical immigrants: those actors who came to America, who failed to achieve stardom, but who remained to help establish North America's theatrical foundations. Although relatively little has been written about those who developed successful careers as actor-managers, many of these contributed more to the American theatre in the first half of the nineteenth century than their highly praised compatriots who came, conquered, and returned to England with their new riches. F.C. Wemyss, whose acting talents were overshadowed by his managerial abilities, guided theatres for a period of almost forty years, mainly in Philadelphia, Baltimore and Pittsburgh. William E. Burton, who had toured with Charles Freer in England and first came to America in 1834, contributed as much to American theatre through his theatrical management in Philadelphia, Baltimore and New York as through his acting talents. James W. Wallack, who first appeared in America as an actor at the Park in 1818, later brought his considerable managerial skills to various New York theatres, especially to the Lyceum and then to his own Wallack's Theatre. Even Henry Preston, who was spending his whole career in failure and obscurity, had offered Tyrone Power to the people of Richmond, Junius Brutus Booth and Edwin Forrest to his Albany audience, and Booth, Vandenhoff, "Yankee" Hill, and Charles Freer to the discerning public of Saint John. Preston's individual contribution to the development of nineteenth-century drama was slight, but his function as actor-manager was central to the theatre of the times.

Charles Freer, whom Preston had first brought to Saint John in 1839, and whose career would follow all three of the theatrical paths outlined above, began acting in England sometime in the 1820s. His name heads the list of the "excellent stock company" with which London's east-end Pavilion theatre opened in 1828.[10] Freer's younger contemporary Henry Turner, in his recollections of the Pavilion's early days, says "the most popular actor at that date was Charles Freer, who was known as 'The Kean of the East.'"[11] This comparison of Freer's style with the hot-blooded acting of Edmund Kean is reinforced by another contemporary, Walter Lacey. Speaking of James Wallack's acting at Drury Lane, he judged that Wallack "was unapproachable in Romantic Drama, although his laurels were hotly contested by . . . Freer at the Pavilion."[12] Other records show that Freer played Sir Giles Overreach at Sadler's Wells in 1830 and Sir Charles Cropland in Coventry in 1834.[13] Almost fifty years after the performances, Turner still remembered the "great excellence" of Freer's Gypsy King and his "suave and elegant Mercutio."[14] In 1831, Freer followed the path taken by Preston and became an actor-manager. His management of London's new Garrick Theatre, however, lasted less than a year, as did his later leadership of that theatre in 1838, and neither attempt brought Freer much success. His strength was in his acting; although he was not invited to tread the boards in the more fashionable west-end London theatres, his Romantic hero found a comfortable home throughout the 1830s in the east-end saloon theatres which operated on the far side both of respectability and legality.

The acting demands of unlicensed east-end London variety stages differed markedly from those of Drury Lane and Covent Garden. Saloon theatres, in which Freer would both rise and fall, demanded a much greater reliance on histrionics than on subtle characterization. At the Pavilion and the Garrick, sensational melodrama was offered to "a populace largely composed of seafaring men, and so numerous, unruly, and uncouth, that one reads occasionally of a boy being trampled to death in the gallery, and of large bottles being flung upon the stage, to the terror of the actors."[15] While neither George Fenety nor Thomas Hill deigned to describe the style of acting which the Saint John and Fredericton audiences so admired in Freer, his theatrical foundations were styled on characterizations like fellow-actor E. F. Saville's "Bill Sikes" on the east-end stage:

> The murder of Nancy was the great scene. Nancy was always dragged round the stage by her hair, and after this effort Sikes always looked up defiantly at the gallery, as he was doubtless told to do in the marked prompt copy. He was always answered by one loud and fearful curse, yelled by the whole mass like a Handel Festival chorus. The curse was answered by Sikes dragging Nancy twice round the stage, and then, like Ajax, defying the lightning. The simultaneous yell then became louder and more blasphemous. Finally, when Sikes, working up to a well rehearsed climax, smeared Nancy with red ochre, and taking her by the hair (a most powerful wig) seemed to dash her brains out on the stage, no explosion of dynamite invented by the modern anarchist, no language ever dreamt of in Bedlam could equal the outburst. A thousand enraged voices, which sounded like ten thousand, with the roar of a dozen escaped menageries, filled the theatre and deafened the audience, and when the smiling ruffian came forward and bowed, their voices in thorough plain English expressed a fierce determination to tear his sanguinary entrails from his sanguinary body.[16]

Such were the east-end London audiences before which the young Freer developed the melodramatic skills he would bring to North America.

By the end of the 1830s, Freer's abilities for high tragedy, like those of Cooke and many others before him, were being weakened by over-indulgence in potent libations. "Mr. Freer," according to one critic, "is intoxicated every evening to the great disgrace of the decent part of the audience and to the detriment of the performance."[17] Drunkeness on stage was only one of his problems; a second developed offstage because of what the same critic delicately calls "matrimonial misadventure." Doubtless, Freer's personal problems and his concommitant fall in public favor figured in his decision to follow the example set by Edmund Kean a decade earlier to offer his thespian skills to a new audience in America.

By the mid 1800s, America's theatrical centre was shifting to New York, and actors who opened in Philadelphia or elsewhere felt the need to prove themselves on the Park Street Theatre stage in New York. Just as the Park stage was the venue for English stars of the first magnitude, so Richard III was the accepted role in which they introduced themselves to America. Cooke had opened as Richard in 1810; Edmund Kean did the same in 1820 and again on his second tour in 1825; Booth opened as Richard in his American *début* in Richmond and in his later New York opening; Charles Kean did likewise at the Park in 1830. Only Macready, "the most chaste, finished and classic actor that had ever graced the American stage,"[18] divorced himself from the common herd by opening as Virginius. (There was, it seems, no end to the appeal of Richard III; the London actress Mrs Henry Lewis was only "one of the first" women to essay the role in America,[19] and a record of sorts must surely have been established when the black depths of Richard's villainy were explored at the Broadway Theatre in 1849 by the presumably precocious Ellen Bateman, aged four.) If Freer wished to show himself the equal of those who had come before him, the role in which to open was obviously Richard III.

That event occurred on May 18, 1839, on the stage of the Park Theatre as part of a benefit for an English actress, Mrs Gibbs. The event caused not a ripple of excitement in the New York audience. Judged by the engagements that followed, Freer's reception was warm but not enthusiastic enough for him to be retained for a season at the Park or offered a tour, like those of his precursors, to Boston, Baltimore and Philadelphia. There is no evidence that Freer returned to the Park's aging boards during his first tour of America, and his diminishing success can be traced by following both his roles and the theatres in which he found work during his first New York season.

The National Theatre, where Freer appeared on May 23, was much newer than the Park, but it would never command the respect in which the Park was held, and it did not survive long enough to develop its own identity. The 1838-39 season, under Wallack's management, had opened with Edwin Forrest playing Othello, Tell, Spartacus and his other familiar roles. Between Forrest's opening and Freer's engagement as Shylock, the theatre had interspersed its offerings of Italian opera with productions starring, among others, Hamblin and Freer's old friend William Burton, with whom he had made his theatrical *début* in Coventry some years earlier. Unfortunately for Freer, it

Freer as Shylock

as Shylock

Freer as the Pilot

as the Pilot.

was the Italian opera, not the tragic drama, which sustained the National's box office, and his run was short. On September 23, with Charles Kean scheduled to play Richard in the evening, the building burned. It was reopened in 1840, but burned again in less than a year. In its brief lifetime, the National's stage had been graced by Booth's Shylock, Kean's Hamlet, and Forrest's Virginius and Richelieu. Its last Shakespeare offerings, two weeks before the second fire, were Booth's Iago, Hamlet and Richard. While Freer's 1839 engagement at the National might have lacked the prestige of his Park opening, this theatre was certainly providing the New York public with those roles by which he hoped to forge his American career.

Unfortunately, this second exposure to the New York audience also failed to kindle any sparks of enthusiasm for the would-be star. Within a week, he was forced to lower his sights and accept employment at two of the city's "minor theatres," the Olympic and the Franklin. The Olympic was "undoubtedly the most popular place of amusement ever known in New York."[20] It had opened in 1837, and it found its theatrical niche by catering to tastes somewhere between the more refined sensibilities of the Park and the delights of the Bowery and the Franklin. Booth's portrayal of Richard was one of the very few Shakespearean offerings extended to the Olympic's audience. Freer's choice of characters at the Olympic shows his willingness to trim his sails to the prevailing winds. He opened on May 27 as Virginius, and continued by portraying Othello, Tell, Sir Giles Overreach, Bertram and Jaffier—"the tragic list as standardised by Forrest (with just a dash of Booth)."[21] Freer's descent from the poetic to the popular heroes was further marked by his roles of Alcouz in *The Pirate's Oath* and Edgard in *The Idiot*. Without a break, Freer moved on to the Franklin, "a little box of a place"[22] which had opened in 1835 and was already nearing the end of its career as a legitimate theatre. Here, on June 10, he once more attempted to scale the heights with his Richard but, the following night, he regressed once more to *The Pirate's Oath*. Two nights later, he was back at the Olympic, which was also "speeding to its doom."[23] Here he ended his season—scarcely a month after opening at the Park Theatre—as Edgard, Shylock, Fitzarden in *The Lear of Private Life* and, on June 19, as Pierre in the forgotten *The Vagrant, His Wife and Family*. Freer's decline had indeed been swift.

Freer's month in New York had raised him to the level of "a faintly twinkling star."[24] Yet, with all the alternatives of North America before him, it is surprising to find him next employed by Henry Preston at Hopley's Theatre in Saint John. Freer's knowledge of eastern Canada might well have come to him from William R. Blake, who had been one of the original managers of the Olympic. Blake had directed the 1837-38 season at the Franklin and, along with his wife, frequently acted at these two theatres. A native of Nova Scotia, Blake had worked in theatre management in Boston, Philadelphia and New York, and had acted with various American and English companies. He had also managed the Pearl Street Theatre in Albany shortly before Henry Preston took it over in 1838. Acquainted with Freer, Preston and the Maritimes' potential, Blake was in a position to advise Preston as that actor-manager developed his first season in New Brunswick. At the same time, Preston hired Mrs Gibbs, at whose benefit Freer's American career had its start a few months earlier. By a simple shift in location and audience, Freer's star was given the opportunity to shine once more.

Preston's 1839 Saint John season, however, offered neither Freer nor anyone else in the company an opportunity to scale the theatrical heights. Records for the period from September to December show that Freer's portrayals of Edgard the Idiot and George Barnwell constituted the most demanding evenings of his engagement. He also played the lead in *Pedlar's Acre*, a script presumably on a par with others of the season's offerings such as *The Golden Farmer*, *The Spoil'd Child*, and *The Fox and the Wolf*.[25] In comparison, the Olympic's season had been caviar to the masses.

At the end of Preston's 1839 Saint John season, Freer returned to the States, where he resumed his American quest for fame and fortune in Philadelphia. The 1839-40 season at Philadelphia's Walnut Street Theatre was characterized by its actor-manager, F.C. Wemyss, as a "slough of despond."[26] The theatre owners forced Wemyss to raise ticket prices by 50%, thus decreasing the size of his audience so severely that on 155 of the season's 261 nights ticket sales recovered less than half of the evening's expenses. Forrest could bring in $398, acting as Virginius, and collect $852 on his benefit. But Freer's friend William Burton averaged only $165 a night and took in $653 on his benefit. Entire weeks went by with total ticket revenues of less than $300. Wemyss could scarcely have been excited by Freer, who opened on May 14, 1840 as Edgard the Idiot, averaged less than $50 a night over four nights, and attracted only $118 on his benefit. Even the aging and embarrassingly sodden Booth, appearing the following month, averaged $117 a night for the frustrated Wemyss. Freer could read the writing on the wall and, perhaps motivated by his knowledge of the fate awaiting failed actors, decided that the time had come for a prudent retreat. His rapid decline to the lesser New York stages, followed by his further descent to the far reaches of provincial theatre, had shown Freer that the success of his countrymen Kean, Booth and Macready was not to be his. His attempt to outflank New York through his engagement at the Walnut Street Theatre had met with faint enthusiasm. His failure to capture fame in America was a disappointment; his failure to capture fortune forced his decision to return to those audiences which had appreciated him. Freer prudently ended his first sojourn in the New World and returned to the theatrical haunts of east-end London.

Freer's first experience of American theatre had taught him the lesson that Preston had already learned. The main prop of professional theatre was the star system. In 1833, a season which the Prestons had probably spent in New York, records for the Park Theatre show that the pattern experienced by Wemyss was not untypical—when a star was featured, box office receipts increased dramatically. Tyrone Power's opening generated $1150, and his thirty-seven performances averaged $480. Charles and Fanny Kemble averaged $732 over forty-five evenings; Charles' farewell benefit brought in $1,456. But the Park company, when acting without the attraction of such stars, averaged scarcely $150.[27] The box office take waxed and waned in America, as it did at Drury Lane and Covent Garden, in concert with the manager's abilities to offer popular stars to his fickle audiences. American theatre managers, unfortunately but almost inevitably, followed the demands of the box office. Except for the occasional lapse into extreme nationalism, evidenced by such events as the Astor Place riot, the audiences of America's premiere theatres showed themselves to be little interested in the development of indigenous drama. A resident company could be called on to mount five or six different productions to accommodate a week's engagement by a touring star. Actors considered rehearsals to be optional exercises in which they did not show off by working too hard; such rehearsals were used mainly to develop traffic patterns which would best leave the sightlines to the star always unhindered. Drastic cutting to leave out parts of plays in which the star was not on stage—the final acts of *The Merchant of Venice* and *Horace*, for instance—were met without a murmur of audience protest even when the truncated plays no longer made sense. The playwright's work was valued as no more than the indifferent instrument through which the audience was offered the opportunity to view a Kean or a Rachel in person.

Freer's return to London did not rekindle the enthusiasm he had once experienced there. The tavern theatres in which he had won a modicum of fame had been reshaped and legitimized by the theatre Licensing Act of 1843, and Freer realized that he, the Kean of the east-end, had somehow lost his London audience. His prospects were now even dimmer in England than they had been in America. Consequently, in 1844, unsoured by his earlier rejection, he repacked his bags and returned to give to North America a second chance. This time he abandoned his former strategy of a frontal assault on the New York stage. Aware of the star system and his own inadequacies in that regard, he had perceived much theatre taking place outside that system, and that—paralleling his London career in the variety entertainments of the tavern theatres—an actor-manager could make a prosperous livelihood by appealing to tastes less elevated than those of the Park Theatre audience. The latter half of the 1840s was a time of transition in the New York theatres. The aging Park burned in 1848, and only the Broadway aspired to take its place. The Olympic's best years were behind it. The Greenwich's days were numbered. The standard tragedies were to be found at the Bowery, but they were well mixed with equestrian drama, melodrama and other popular entertainments. The Chatham, which took on the old National's name, generally offered scripts of only minor interest. But, by the decade's end, managers of the Chatham, the Olympic and the new Burton's Theatre discovered that New Yorkers would flock to plays about themselves. The English near-monopoly on scripts and actors was weakening. Significantly, American morality plays began to draw audiences which had until then viewed the theatre as a tool of the devil. In 1850, the epitome of the genre, *The*

Freer as Alonzo

Drunkard, would play at the Bowery, at the National, and at a new "lecture room" opened for the production of moral domestic dramas in Barnum's Museum. American drama was beginning to discover its own identity, and Freer's sense of the potential offered by such theatres was well placed.

While Preston was attempting to escape poverty in Saint John's and rock throwers in Charlottetown, Freer began his second New York offensive much better prepared for the reality of that city's commercial theatre. He did not attempt to open at the Park, but instead appeared at the Chatham, a popular, though uninspiring, playhouse which had been opened in 1839. His sojourn in England had obviously provided him with opportunity not only to act but also to write, for on his opening nights at the Chatham, October 7 and 8, he provided the New York audience with a "judicious and natural" performance as the lead in his own version of *The Gipsy King*.[28] Acting with him in the production was Mrs Preston, the recently decamped wife of Henry Preston, who had returned to New York from Newfoundland to continue her career as a stock actress. Almost immediately, Freer added a third string to his bow by becoming the Chatham's stage manager.

Freer's 1844-45 season as actor, playwright and stage-manager at the Chatham showed how completely he was willing to mold his performances to the audience at hand. *The Spirit of the Times*, a New York newspaper, records productions of at least two more of Freer's own scripts, *True Blue* and *The Drover Boy*, and describes the latter as "well written and effective." Along with his own scripts, Freer offered such *opi* as *The Corn Laws of England* and *Mandalzar the Accursed*. The newspaper critic termed Freer "an actor of much taste, feeling, and delicate conception" for his Scrooge in *A Christmas Carol*. His Hamlet was acknowledged to be "a few shades above the ordinary level." However, the season's quality was not universally admired: *Mandalzar the Accursed* was flayed for being "not only badly written, and stupidly contrived, but shockingly blasphemous." This same paper's irate criticism of *The Monks of Monks Hall* shows that while Freer's taste might not always have been elevated, his reading of his audience was accurate: the "stupid and vulgar play . . . instead of receiving a decided rebuke, has attracted good houses, much to the disgrace of the management and its patrons." Freer interspersed among these literary monuments to poor taste such crowd-pleasing performers as Booth, Rice and "Yankee" Hill, but, despite this talent, his season was only modestly successful. On April 26, 1845, he took his benefit and surrendered the Chatham to others. He moved back to his old haunt, the Olympic, on April 29, for *The Moment of Terror or The Corsair's Revenge*. But this theatre ended its season the following night, and Freer found himself once more at liberty.

Freer's need for employment was matched by Preston's need for a lead actor. On July 19, the Saint John *Courier* reported that Preston "had dispatched his agent to the principal American Theatres" in order to strengthen his company. The *Provincial Association* tumult and the acting talents of Miss McBride had not been sufficient to disguise the fact that the company was in need of a strong male tragedian. Answering the call, and setting aside for the present time his managerial ambitions, Freer once more headed out to the northern theatrical provinces. Just as he had earlier shaped his offerings to the strengths of Miss McBride, Preston now turned to those scripts which, while providing some scope for Miss McBride's limited talents, would allow Freer to "make his appearance immediately in some of those majestic characters in which he shines so transcendently conspicuous."[29] Thus Freer, possibly for the last time in his entire career, was being given the opportunity that had been denied him by the audiences of New York's Chatham Theatre—the opportunity to act before an appreciative public in the masculine classics of the mid-1800s: *Tell, The Hunchback, Virginius, Pizarro* and, for a note of culture, *Othello, Macbeth,* and *A New Way to Pay Old Debts.* Once again Freer found himself receiving the respect he sought. At his first appearance, the *Courier* exclaimed, "This admirable actor's fame has been established in the British Theatres, and lost nothing by his personation of the patriotic TELL."[30] His Othello, playing to packed houses, was "a masterpiece of delineation."[31] Even Fenety, who earlier claimed to have avoided theatre, was seduced by the talents of the English tragedian:

We looked in at the theatre on Friday evening [August 29] and saw FREER in 'Pizarro.' It was the first time that we had the pleasure of seeing this gentleman; and we must say that he is a splendid fellow; indeed we did not think he was the performer he is. We have seen Forrest, Macready, Kean, J.R. Scott, Wallack, and several others of the first water—and we must say we like Freer.[32]

as Iago in Othello

Freer as Iago
in *Othello*

For his benefit at the end of the summer, he had sufficient confidence in the tastes of the Saint John audience to risk *Macbeth*. This performance brought to the theatre, in Fenety's phrase, "the *elite* and *beauty* of the city."[33] When Freer had first played at the Walnut Street Theatre in Philadelphia, in 1840, the stage manager (and later theatre historian) Charles Durang had described him as "a very excellent melo-dramatic actor, who had a good deal of the elegant dash about him."[34] The intervening years in London, if they had not allowed his talents to develop, had not diminished his skills.

Basking in Freer's reflected glory were both Preston and Miss McBride. Preston had had to take leading roles opposite McBride early in the summer, and he had not fared badly at the hands of the local critics. As the Stranger, he was "the very misanthrope."[35] At the end of the season, another letter gushed over him as an actor whose "versatile genius, like his prototype Garrick, fits him for almost any character in the whole range of the Drama."[36] And even Fenety's *Morning News* allowed that "Preston always excels in what he undertakes."[37] Preston felt no grief in giving up the acting spotlight to Freer. But, obviously, as Freer's star had waxed, Miss McBride's had also waned. Denied productions of those scripts which showed the female lead to best advantage, she was forced to make do with roles which, while not insubstantial, offered less centre stage time than those she had taken before Freer arrived. For her benefit at the end of the summer she was faced with the quandary of choosing a production in which her female lead would play second star to Freer—thus assuring herself of a bumper house—or choosing a script in which Freer could be assigned a role somewhat beneath her own, with the concomitant risk that such an evening would attract a smaller audience. Her creative solution was to offer *As You Like It*, in which her Rosalind could shine unchallenged opposite one of the gentleman amateurs, while Freer (as Jacques) could also have his moment on centre stage. It was undoubtedly the best she could make of a bad situation, but it did not make her happy. Preston was glad to see her leave the company soon afterwards.

Saint John might not have been able to support indefinitely the heights of classic tragedy, but Preston's season had offered Freer much more respectable roles than those he had been able to play during his recent New York engagement. Wishing to capitalize on his star's popularity, Preston's mind turned once more to the theatrical audience he had developed, and then abandoned, in Fredericton. Mindful of the bailiff who had ended his winter season there prematurely, Preston turned to Freer, with his experience as an actor-manager, to lead a company back up river to the capital at the end of the summer. One more time, Freer had the opportunity to exhibit those talents which, while inadequate to the demands of the Park Theatre, were more than sufficient to evoke the approbation of the New Brunswick audience. During the week of September 10, 1845, he offered the Fredericton audience his Virginius, the Stranger, Iago, Tell and, for his benefit in this largely British setting, Richard III. Thomas Hill welcomed this "Kean of the east" with open arms:

> Mr. Freer is an excellent actor,—we cannot say faultless, but certainly one of the best who has ever made his appearance in this Province. His ennunciation is good, and the whole of his reading is beautifully correct. His greatest fault is, in our opinion, too great a volubility in the exciting parts. We did not witness his William Tell, but we liked his Stranger, and his Iago still better: but perhaps his masterpiece is Richard the Third. In this popular character he drew down tremendous applause, although we may say almost wholly unsupported, for the Americans who personated the other characters knew just as much of playing English Kings, Queens, and Noblemen as a cow does of a sanctuary.[38]

Freer's triumph carried through a second week in Fredericton, ending with Sheridan's *Pizarro* on September 22. During the week, he obviously spent time with Thomas Hill, talking of his plans or, more precisely, his dreams for his career. A week later, the *Loyalist* carried an account of Freer's idea for setting up an Atlantic provinces circuit, a project in which Henry Preston had been unprofitably engaged for a number of years, under the experienced management of that actor-manager of the London and New York stages, Charles Freer.

> Mr. Freer has been exceedingly well received in [Fredericton], as well as in Saint John, and we have reason to believe not many weeks will elapse before he will return to this Province. We believe that it is in contemplation to establish a *Provincial* Company, who will chiefly depend for support on St. John and Halifax. We like the plan . . . and of all theatrical characters who have visited us lately we do not hesitate to say Mr. Freer is the proper person to be entrusted with the management.[39]

Such an endorsement must have come as a surprise to Preston, who had been enjoying Hill's support since he had established himself in Fredericton the previous December. Freer, however, could not have taken his discussion with the *Loyalist* editor too seriously. At the end of his Fredericton engagement, he packed his bags and turned back to the American stages, never to return.

Notes

1. Ireland, I, 145.
2. Ireland, I, 271.
3. Don B. Wilmeth, *George Frederick Cooke: Machiavel of the Stage* (Wesport, Conn.: Greenwood Press, 1980), 259.
4. Ireland, I, 274. Cooke's recent biographers have treated his last years less superficially and, as a result, more sympathetically than nineteenth-century theatre historians. Yet Arnold Hare admits that it was Cooke's pattern of drunkeness and sobriety that led him "to a lonely death in exile" [*George Frederick Cooke: the Actor and the Man* (Bath: Pitman Press, 1980), 5].
5. Wilmeth substantiates his assessment of Cooke's "triumph" by providing a table of box office receipts for the actor's American performances, 291-94.
6. Clapp, 176.
7. Raymund FitzSimons, *Edmund Kean* (London: Hamish Hamilton, 1976), 148.
8. Ireland, I, 483.
9. Brown, I, 322, 300, 102.
10. A.E. Wilson, *East End Entertainment* (London: Arthur Barker Ltd., 1954), 68.
11. Henry Turner, "Random Recollections," *The Theatre* (September 1, 1885), 146.
12. Walter Lacey, quoted in *Actors and Actresses of Great Britain and the United States,* ed. Matthews and Hutton (New York: Cassell and Company, 1886), III, 69.
13. W. Davenport Adams, *A Dictionary of the Drama* (London: Chatto & Windus, 1904), I, 549; T. Allston Brown, *History of the American Stage* (New York: Dick and Fitzgerald, 1870), 134.
14. Turner, 147.
15. Percy Allen, *The Stage Life of Mrs Stirling* (London: T. Fisher Unwin, 1922), 30.
16. Quoted in Allen, 30.

17. Wilson, 107.
18. Ireland, I, 506.
19. Brown, I, 47.
20. Brown, I, 264.
21. Odell, IV, 315.
22. Brown, I, 257.
23. Odell, IV, 315.
24. Odell, IV, 315.
25. Performance calendar information is taken from Smith.
26. Information concerning this season is taken from F.C. Wemyss, *Twenty-Six Years in the Life of an Actor and Manager* (New York: Burgess, Stringer and Company, 1847), 319-25.
27. The box-office figures are from Ireland, II, 85.
28. Quotations concerning Freer's 1844-45 New York season are taken from Odell, V, 114-16.
29. *Morning News,* July 25, 1845.
30. *Courier,* July 26, 1845.
31. *Courier,* August 9, 1845.
32. *Morning News,* September 1, 1845.
33. *Morning News,* September 3, 1845.
34. Durang, 167.
35. *Chronicle,* July 4, 1845.
36. *Chronicle,* September 5, 1845.
37. *Morning News,* September 8, 1845.
38. *Loyalist,* September 18, 1845.
39. *Loyalist,* September 25, 1845.

Chapter Five

According to Thomas Hill, Charles Freer's departure from New Brunswick in the fall of 1845 was occasioned by the necessity of his returning to New York where "we understand he has an engagement."[1] The engagement, if there was one, has gone unmentioned by the New York theatre historians. But the Maritime circuit that Freer had discussed with Hill during his engagement in Fredericton in 1845 was totally impractical. A brief talk with Preston when the company returned to Saint John would have apprised Freer of the disastrous potential of a Maritime circuit at this time. Despite his years of commitment to the region, Preston's own days in eastern Canada were numbered. Before the year's end, he would be forced to turn south in an attempt to escape those fates which seemed to dog his every venture. Freer chose to do the same.

Freer's two weeks in Fredericton had provided him with his last opportunity to act the heroic roles upon which he had wished to found his career. In the New York to which he returned, such roles were performed before the audiences at the Park and Bowery theatres. At the Park, in the 1846-47 season, Charles Kean essayed *Two Gentlemen of Verona* and *King John*, while Edwin Forrest performed as Lear, Hamlet, Othello and Richelieu. Mrs Mowatt offered her Juliet, and Susan Dennin, who had acted with Freer in Preston's 1845 New Brunswick company, played Prince Arthur to Kean's King John. At the Bowery Theatre, mingled among the melodramas and comedies, were the very roles for which Freer felt himself most suited: the Stranger, Virginius, Hamlet, Macbeth, Richelieu and Lear.

Freer, however, was experienced enough by now to subdue his own ambition and, when he took over as manager of the Greenwich, to offer that theatre's audience the fare it desired. Consequently, in the 1846 summer season, Freer mounted a selection of his own scripts, *The Gipsy King*, *True Blue* and *The Drover Boy*, along with such ephemera as *Washington's Birthday*, *Black Eagle*, and *Michael the Ferryman*. The season never aspired beyond *The Stranger*. Management was more inclined to move in the opposite direction:

> Some idea of the subterfuges indulged in by this management may be had from observing that A Pleasant Neighbour figures in the bills for August 18th as The Merry Cobbler, and on the 21st as The Cottage of Content; a piece acted on July 27th as Industry and Union became on August 19th The Incendiary. We know it was the same play because on both occasions Freer was cast for Pierre Maillard.[2]

This summer season may have been beneath critical notice because of its low-brow quality, but it was a success when judged by the one criterion of interest to a theatre manager, the box office receipts. "Though he had lowered the standard of the plays produced," observes Odell, "he had at least kept the house open for over two months." Especially at the Greenwich Theatre, this was the very definition of successful management.

Freer remained manager of the Greenwich for a short fall season. His old aspirations for legitimate theatre had not been entirely smothered, for he opened his new season by acting in *The Lady of Lyons*, *Romeo and Juliet*, and *Pizarro*. Such offerings, while not calculated to strike panic into the hearts of the competition at the Park and the Bowery, were an attempt to rise above the level established during his summer season. Freer's ideals were commendable, but the realities of producing for the populist Greenwich soon brought him back to reality, so that by October he again offered the undemanding fare of *Green Bushes*, *True Blue*, and *The Brigand*. Excitement reached its only peak at the theatre on September 19, when an arsonist was unsuccessful in his attempt to end Freer's season prematurely.[3] Freer's final season as an actor-manager in America, or at least the last recorded in any detail, can be summed up in a single sentence: "No novelties were produced, and the company was so poorly balanced and so wretchedly patronized, that its efforts were utterly wasted."[4] After October 21, 1846, there is "no further record of Freer's activities at this ill-fated house."[5]

Freer's last days in New York are, like his first days, shrouded in mystery. The Greenwich Theatre building began as the Richmond Hill Theatre, had been converted into a saloon, had next become the National Theatre, and, after rebuilding in 1846, was known as the Greenwich Theatre. It then rose one last time

Freer as Count Theodore

Freer as Octavian

from the ashes of its own failures to open, on February 8, 1847, as The New York Opera House. Neither changes of name nor renovations could transform this unfavored establishment into a successful theatre. With Freer as manager, the building survived for one more year, was abandoned in April 1848, and was pulled down in 1849.[6] The historians Ireland and Odell describe a different ending to Freer's second American odyssey. Ireland has Freer figuring "frequently" as one of the "stars" at the Chatham Theatre in the 1846-47 season.[7] Odell notes that Freer returned to the Chatham on February 1, 1847, "for a farewell visit 'prior to his departure for Europe.'"[8] In this final week "of course he acted his popular Gipsy King," and also his *True Blue or The Seabird's Home* and *Murderer's Leap*. On his final night, February 5, 1847, he rose to the heights of Jaffier, in *Venice Preserved*. "With this," Odell eulogizes, "he departed."

Whether Freer left for England following this engagement, or whether he managed the old Greenwich Theatre through its final transformation as The New York Opera House, is immaterial. His star had run its American course. Now in his late forties, his chance of following his compatriots' lead to theatrical fame and fortune lay behind him. Behind him also were the opportunities to contribute substantially, like other English actor-managers, to the development of American theatre. Before him remained the only course for the failed actor, subsistence through minor roles and crowd-swelling. To meet this fate, Charles Freer returned to east-end London. Henry Turner remembers him:

> Some time in the forties, I saw him play, at the Victoria Theatre, the chief part in "The Bohemians of Paris," and followed by "Macbeth" as an afterpiece (!), wherein he enacted the ambitious Thane. But he was at this date merely a wreck of his former self.[9]

None of the principal chroniclers of the London minor theatres, such as Nicholson, Scott or Richardson, even mentions Freer.

An undated begging note from Freer to a fellow actor, T[homas?] P[otter?] Cooke, substantiates Turner's assessment of Freer's decline from the London stage.

> Dear Sir,
>
> I hope your well known friendly feeling to unfortunate members of the profession will excuse the liberty I have taken in thus addressing you, for the last 3 years I have been signally unfortunate, After struggling to make it pay, I was obliged to

give up my Public House to Brewer and distiller. I went out literally penniless, having lost everything I had been working hard for for years . . . I went to Scotland and was laid up by Rheumatic pains and ague for nearly 16 months, within the last month I have had another severe attack, that has rendered me incapable of acting for the present . . . After 28 years hard toil and servitude, I find myself without the means of bare existence. . . .[10]

Judging by the draft response penciled in on the bottom of Freer's letter, Cooke was able to offer the suffering actor no more than his sympathy.

Four other letters written by Freer to various theatrical connections during his final London years not only record his own pathetic end but stand as primary evidence of the fate that awaited the failed talents who spent their declining years, if not their entire lives, supporting their theatrical betters.[11] Freer's forthright admissions about his own pitiful condition underscore the misery that was the lot of many in his profession.

Of the four letters, one is undated, two are dated, and a newspaper obituary glued to the fourth suggests that it might have been received around the time of his death. The first of the dated letters is headed "Kilby's, 18 Gibraltar Walk, Church Street, Shoreditch March 26, 1855." In it, Freer requests of a "dear friend" named Tom a second loan which will enable him, "in the cheapest way," to travel to Glasgow, where he has the offer of "short" employment. The last half of the letter reflects Freer's wretched state:

I really am ashamed to ask you, dear old friend, after your late prompt kindness to me to assist me a little further by an additional loan of 10/- to be repaid *before I leave Glasgow* for London. I have tried every source I thought likely to assist me, without troubling you, but met with nothing but broken promises and disappointments. I *have* been a great favorite in Glasgow, and I dont think they have forgotten me, it may lead to something better, if without inconveniencing yourself you can oblige me, I shall feel bound to consider it a debt of honor, paramount to anything in its repayment. I would have waited on you today, but am laid up with rheumatic gout in my right foot and [it] confines me to my bed for a day or two, anxiety and walking so much the last few days brought it on. I must leave on Wednesday morning, being one of the cheap train days, therefore dear Tom, if you *will* secure me, let me hear from you in course of tomorrow Tuesday, if favorable, will you send a P.O. order payable in Bethnal Green road to Charles Freer, in return I will send you an I.O.U. for the two sums advanced.

Yours truly and obliged
Charles Freer

In the following year and a half, Freer's fortunes deteriorated until he was barely able to keep body and soul together. A letter dated "Aug 15 / 56" shows that he was now forced to lean, not only on his friends, but on anyone with whom he had any hope of success. In this letter, Freer reaches back seventeen years for a connection to John Sinclair. On the evening of May 18, 1839, at New York's Park Theatre, Mrs Gibbs had appeared for her benefit performance as Maria, opposite Sinclair as Frederick in the operetta *No*. It was at this benefit that Freer made his New York debut as Richard III; he would not have forgotten it, and he hoped that Sinclair would remember it, too. Freer's theme, once again, is the fate of souls who, in a world with neither security nor pensions, find themselves unneeded.

Sir, Pray pardon the liberty taken by an old actor of 30 years standing for thus addressing you, also a comparative stranger with the exception of being introduced some years ago to you, by W. Burton, & playing one night at the Park Theatre for Mrs Gibbs' Benefit—my object in addressing you now is to ask the obligation of a little pecuniary assistance & however small it will be gratefully remembered. From failure in [business?] pecuniary & domestic losses, long & painful illnesses, the necessary consequences following poverty & want of engagements—I have for the last 3 years endured the cruelest privations, until misfortune has reached its culminating point, and I am so completely Hors de Combat as to be without the means of even procuring food—I am striving if possible, to get out to N. York once again & take whatever offers—if Sir you will grant a trifle for necessity of present life it will be most acceptable—again apologising for this liberty

I beg to remain
Your Very Obt. Servt.
Charles Freer

London Theatres

Wedy aftn.

Bower
Saloon

My dear B.

Will you lend
me from Keril 3 or 5 Shillings
just to carry on till next
Tuesday, when I have a
Benefit at this place, the
only chance I have of
paying myself, I have a
clean share, I have been
here nearly 3 weeks and
reced only 10/- altogether, which
after paying lodgings, has
left me half Starved, if
convenient pray oblige me,
I will wait for you at the
House I last saw you near
Hungerford Market

and pardon this liberty taken.

by Yours truly obleged

Charles Feer

I have enclosd you an
order for Tuesday night
it will be sure to be admitted

Theatrical employment, in these final years, was scarcely sufficient to keep Freer from death's door. The polished phrasing of the above letter suggests that much thought had gone into its composition. Freer introduces himself by way of Burton and Gibbs, he enters his plea with telling detail, and takes humble leave with whatever dignity he can muster as one theatrical personage talking to another. The letter's formal elegance creates almost a sense of distance between its author and his desperate condition. The final address, "London Theatres," adds a subtle touch which manages to suggest that, while momentarily disadvantaged, Freer remains a practicing actor. But in the third of the four letters, a short note to "My dear B," any attempt at dignity or elegance has been abandoned, and it becomes obvious that Freer has only one immediate concern: his survival in a profession where, even when he can find work, he is not paid enough to keep himself alive. In stark, ungrammatical prose, he admits that he is actually starving to death.

Wedy Aftn
Bower Saloon

My dear B,
Will you lend a poor devil 3 or 5 shillings just to carry on till next Tuesday, when I have a Benefit at this place, the only chance I have of paying myself, I have a clear share. I have been here nearly 3 weeks and recd. only 10/- altogether, which, after paying lodgings, has left me half-starved. If convenient pray oblige me. I will wait for you at the House I last saw you near Hungerford Markets. And pardon this liberty taken by

Yours truly obliged
Charles Freer

I have enclosed you an order for Tuesday night. It will be *sure* to be admitted

The seriousness of Freer's situation is reinforced by his address. The Bower Saloon, or the "sour balloon" as it was locally known, in Lambeth, offered "mixed entertainment for local audiences and employment for out-of-work professionals and semi-amateurs."[12] Lacking more than rudimentary lighting, and possessed of one built-in set of a Swiss village, it flavored its offerings of melodrama with ballad opera, dog dramas, sing-songs and fireworks. Hungerford Market was home to the New Music Hall, a building described as a "seedy" place with a "damp, tunnel-like atmosphere which not even the fumes of tobacco, grog, and gas could overpower."[13]

The last of the four letters is addressed to a "Mr. Gardiner," obviously a theatrical associate who had access to the head of a theatrical company of which Freer had once been a part. Freer's reticence as to his reason for wishing to rejoin the company could well be based on the embarrassment of having to acknowledge the simple fact that he needed the money to buy food.

Dear Friend,

Since I parted from you, I have received a parcel by Caswell's Coach—in it, a letter which letter & another reason has determined me to make an advance towards reconciliation with Mr Linley—as to staying—to that if you will again use your friendly offices as mediator twixt us twain I will thank you— therefore ask Mr L. if he is willing to admit me again into his Company—if so, I am willing to return my *allegiance*. You will smile at my seeming irresolution but I assure you candidly I *have* a particular reason—let me know Mr Linley's determination on a scrap of paper by the person who brings this as I shall then know how to act—Say what you think consistent with honorable feeling to Mr L & you echo mine—

Yours truly
J.C. Freer

This letter is undated, but in its top corner a thin newspaper clipping has been glued, announcing in very small print, that "— Mr. Charles Freer, the old East end favourite, died, under painful circumstances, Dec. 23, 1857." Ireland enlarges on these "painful circumstances": "He committed suicide in London, about the 1st of January, 1858, while in poverty and distress, resulting from a lack of employment."[14] The death occurred, according to Henry Turner, "in a coffee house near Westminster Bridge."[15] Freer was about 55 years old.

Charles Freer's suicide ended an insignificant life. While this scarcely noticed actor, and others like him, provided the background against which the era's stars were able to shine so brightly, theatrical chroniclers have been preoccupied with those few stars rather than with the theatrical firmament in which their stardom was possible. Yet Freer's varied career, from his early successes at the Park to his years as an actor-manager and his end in the typical poverty and wretchedness

86

of the unrewarded actor, includes more of the mid-nineteenth century theatrical experience than do the lives of his more successful confreres. His brief letters, because they document the misery experienced by so many who were committed to the acting profession, express the social reality of nineteenth-century theatre more accurately than do the memoirs of those actors and managers who, having achieved fame and fortune on the stage, had time and money to retire and sing the praises of the theatrical life from the sheltered warmth of secure old age.

Notes

1. *Loyalist,* September 25, 1845.
2. Odell, V, 222.
3. Brown, I, 236.
4. Ireland, II, 279-80.
5. Odell, V, 297.
6. Brown, I, 236.
7. Ireland, II, 478.
8. Ireland, V, 281.
9. Turner, 146.
10. I am indebted to Dorothy Swerdlove, of the New York Public Library, for making this letter available to me. Though undated, the situation described in this letter suggests that it was written before the letters following. It was written at "Plumstead near Woolwich, Kent."
11. I am indebted to the Harvard Theatre Collection for permission to publish these four letters.
12. Mollie Sands, *Robson of the Olympic* (London: The Society for Theatre Research, 1979), 19.
13. Harold Scott, *The Early Doors* (London: Nicholson & Watson, 1946), 143.
14. Ireland, II, 270.
15. Turner, 147.

Chapter Six

Henry Preston's dream of theatrical success in the Maritimes had been encouraged by the success of his short season in Fredericton in the fall of 1845. His troupe was by now quite strong, despite Fenety's criticism that they were "anything but creditable to Preston's taste."[1] Charles Freer, schooled in the traditions of London's east end, was equally at home in heroic tragedy and melodrama. Miss McBride, who had been a dancer, singer and company actress on the Boston and New York stages for the previous twenty years, had been at least adequate in comedy if not in tragedy. J.P. Addams, though his skills would never equal those of his more famous theatrical brother, A.A. Addams, possessed sufficient talent to carry on as an actor and minor playwright in both America and Australia until his death in Boston in the 1880s. Susan and Kate Dennin, only eleven and nine years old at this time, would soon establish themselves in New York, pursue their careers in theatres from Boston to San Francisco and then, like Addams, travel on to Australia and back. This mixture of experienced and youthful professionals from the American stage suggests that Preston, though working far from New York and Boston, was sufficiently in touch with the major centres to draw together a respectable company.

Preston's own success in Fredericton before his undignified midnight retreat, coupled with the rather uneven success of his spring and summer seasons in Saint John, gave him the optimism once more to throw caution to the wind and fit up a new Saint John theatre. The success of Freer's September return to Fredericton must have reinforced his vision of the theatrical potential of New Brunswick. So, although the members of his summer's troupe gradually drifted back to the States, Preston mustered enough support for a fall season in Saint John. However, he was not to escape the pattern of disasters that had followed him from Virginia to Newfoundland.

Since the spring of 1844, Preston had retreated from Newfoundland, he had been stoned on Prince Edward Island, and he had been chased out of Fredericton. Tied by the fates to such a wheel of misfortunes, the long-suffering actor-manager could not have been totally surprised to wake up on the morning of December 5, 1845, to the news that his new theatre had been destroyed by fire. The *Courier* blamed the conflagration on "the careless and inefficient manner" in which the building's stove pipes had been installed.[2] But Fenety's *Morning News* hinted at a darker motivation:

> That a spirit of Hostility against the Theatre has of late prevailed among ill-disposed persons, cannot be denied, but to suppose that anyone could be found in the community fiendish enough to destroy it is a matter that must rest with the opinion of those who can account for the thing in no other way.[3]

Whether by arson or by accident, Preston had lost not only his theatre, but also his uninsured scenery, his wardrobe, his properties and his books. "Many a long month," Fenety wrote sympathetically, "had he laboured assiduously, and in the face of many obstacles, to accomplish his object, and when the greatest of his difficulties were surmounted, down comes the hand of affliction to lay low all the fruits of his exertions!" Preston was faced with a choice between abandoning the theatre altogether and starting over still again. Rallied by whatever strengths supported him at similar junctures in the past, and by the ever-faithful Miss Hildreth, Preston chose to persevere. Like Thomas Hill, who found it impossible to choose any vocation in life other than journalism, Preston seems never to have considered seriously the possibility of pursuing a career more promising than the life of a provincial theatrical impresario. As surely as Hill would return to his troubled partnership with Doak, Preston's loyalties bound him to the stage.

After his Saint John theatre burned, the long-suffering actor-manager shouldered his remaining belongings and, accompanied by Miss Hildreth, he left New Brunswick for the last time. Preston's circuit had always taken him from Saint John to Halifax; probably guided more by instinct than enthusiasm, he once again headed for the Nova Scotia capital. By the end of February, 1846, he had begun his winter season. While the *Nova Scotian* applauded the couple's acting talent, Preston's situation was not hopeful: "The company laboured under the several disadvantages of a first night, and want of more properties."[4] His theatrical belongings had been lost and his company was now decimated. After his Halifax season, Preston shook the dust of the Maritimes from his shoes forever.

It is difficult to say whether Preston was guided by theatrical judgment or simply by instinct during his remaining decade as an actor-manager. The ruin of his Maritime venture no doubt took its toll on both his enthusiasm and his energy, but the loss had been no greater than that endured six years earlier with the failure of his Albany theatre. After that earlier defeat, he had picked himself up and begun to look for new and promising theatrical ventures. However, after his Maritime disaster, he lacked this willingness to search for new horizons. Having chosen to stay in theatre, he would spend the rest of his life revisiting the scenes of his various failures.

Retracing those steps which had first led him to eastern Canada in 1839, Preston and Miss Hildreth moved back to Albany in 1846. Here, he hoped to be kindly remembered by "his old friends and patrons of the late Pearl St. Theatre."[5] He attempted to organize a new theatre and company in Albany, and, indeed, a new company did rise from his efforts. But, curiously, Preston's name was not mentioned in the advertisements for Albany's Broadway Odeon when it opened in February, 1847. Possibly he had lost the company even before it was fully organized. That he somehow remained active there even without his own theatre to manage is shown in a notice in the *Albany Journal* for January 26, 1847: "It will be seen that the friends of Mr. Preston, an old and worthy actor, well known as a manager in former times, when the Drama flourished in Albany, have gotten up for him a Benefit. . . . " The "old and worthy actor" remained in Albany until the summer, at which time he moved down to New York City and attempted to mount a season at one of that city's shabbier theatres, the Greenwich.[6] Charles Freer had managed that theatre the previous year, but neither Freer nor his former manager were able to slow the Greenwich's decline. Preston's efforts were so slight they have gone almost unnoticed by the New York theatre historians.

During the next few years, Preston's name surfaced only sporadically in the pages of various newspapers. He spent the winter of 1847-48 back in Charleston, S.C., attempting to reverse the diminishing fortunes of that city's theatre, but he had arrived there just as Charleston theatre "had reached another period of decay."[7] He managed to keep his theatre going through the winter, until it closed down at the end of March, 1848. By the summer of 1850, he could be found once more touring in small towns, such as Whitehall, in upstate New York. He then crossed into Vermont and set up his company of a dozen actors in Burlington. His month there is illustrative of the continuing problems plaguing him. During his first two weeks, his inadequate financial resources permitted him to offer only readings, rather than full productions, of those plays he had so many times performed. Despite the wholesomeness of his offerings, which ranged from the middle-class respectability of *The Stranger, The Lady of Lyons,* and *Black-eyed Susan* to the culturally irreproachable *Hamlet, Othello,* and *Richard III,* Preston found himself facing those New England forces which still considered theatre the devil's tool. Handbills were posted, under cover of darkness and anonymity, railing against the immoral spirit which had invaded Burlington. The local *Free Press* felt called upon to defend the integrity of Preston's offerings:

> The excellent character of the dramatic exhibitions selected by Mr. Preston, and the highly respectable deportment of the members of the Company, have won the respect and patronage of every community they have visited. They furnish that portion of the drama which "holds the mirror up to nature," without the licentious accompaniments which are too often found in our cities, and which constitute the great objection to modern Theaters.[8]

The editorial defender continued, in an argument with antecedents in Plato and Aristotle, that Preston's troupe provided entertainments that were not only "instructive" and "interesting," but were managed with "propriety and decorum." As had been the case in Fredericton and elsewhere, a hint of success on the horizon then led Preston to gamble his box office takings in a renovation of the Concert Hall which would allow him to offer his supportive audience full productions. His courtship of Burlington's fastidious public for a further two weeks was marred at the end of September by an incident that illustrates the extent to which a company actor, or, more especially, a company actress, was at the continual mercy of the actor-manager:

> Mrs George Melville finding herself seriously involved and utterly destitute of the means to extricate herself in consequence of the failure on the part of Mr. H.W. Preston to fulfill the contract entered into with her professionally, either as regards the payment of her salary or Benefit. Mrs Melville therefore (in

justice to herself and the community) entirely withdraws from all connection with a management in which she has not the slightest confidence, and by whom she has been so deeply wronged. Determined (even though unprotected and alone) to leave Burlington with an untainted name, and depending on the generosity of the Ladies and Gentlemen of Burlington and vicinity, [she will offer a public reading of] the *Merchant of Venice*.[9]

Preston prudently decided not to respond to this published slur on his character and, instead, quietly persevered in Burlington until the middle of October. Then, having exhausted the theatrical potential of the town, Preston had no choice but to move on. When he arrived in Montreal two weeks later, the affronted Mrs Melville (who presumably lacked any immediate alternative) was once more a member of his company.

Oddly enough, Preston's productions in Burlington featured "Mrs H. W. Preston, the celebrated Tragic actress from the Baltimore and Philadelphia Theatres." Preston had, once again, added matrimony to the list of uncharted seas over which he was passing. The faithful Miss Hildreth, who had suffered at Preston's side through his last years in the Maritimes and his unsuccessful return to Albany, had apparently decided to pursue the spectre of her own success alone. In January, 1847, she had acted in a benefit for Preston in Albany, but soon thereafter she began to reappear on the New York stage, where she was "cast for anything."[10] She might well be the same Miss Hildreth who married Charles Freer's old actor-manager friend William. E. Burton and disappeared from the theatrical records around 1850.[11] Her place was taken, at least for the moment, by Mrs Isabella Preston.

Preston's month in Montreal brought no change in his fortunes. Although his introductory advertisement listed a company of sixteen actors, the Montreal *Gazette* mentions that he had "opened the theatre under unfavorable circumstances, with but a part of his company, and without due preparation."[12] The "part of his company" with which he had opened was most likely—as had been the case in Halifax—all the company he had. The Burlington season had shown that Preston obviously was leading a troupe who had known better times. The *Gazette*'s criticisms that Preston's own acting left something to be desired and that not all actors had committed their roles to memory suggest that the old actor-manager had underestimated the critical sensibilities of the Montreal audience. He quickly realized his company's quality was not acceptable, left the troupe in the hands of his wife, and traveled south in search of more talented actors. The inadequacy that worried Preston can easily be seen by the range of characters (of both sexes) his wife had been called upon to personate: Mrs Haller in *The Stranger*, Claude Melnotte in *The Lady of Lyons*, and Bassanio in *The Merchant of Venice*. Unfortunately, the new actors Preston could afford to hire were not sufficiently talented to change the course of his fortunes in Montreal. His season lasted only from late October until December, 1850, and left no greater record of success than any of the other ventures he mounted in the years following his disastrous Saint John fire.

Over the next year and a half, Preston must have faced the fact that he had achieved little in his theatrical lifetime. In 1851 or early 1952 his touring company disbanded, his second wife, Isabella, left him and returned to the potentially-prosperous theatrical centres of Boston and New York, and the aging manager attempted, one more time, to escape his aimless wandering by setting up a permanent theatre in the city where he had felt his warmest welcome, Albany. The Green Street Theatre, Albany's first theatre building, had been erected in 1811, used as a church from 1819 until 1851, and reconverted to a theatre in 1852.[13] Preston formed a new company, leased this theatre, and opened for business on July 5, 1852. The old building was to be the old actor's his last battlefield in his war against the theatrical fates.

Preston opened the theatre before the necessary renovations were completed—a sign of either his enthusiasm or his lack of credit. When he tested the waters by taking his first benefit a week later, the *Albany Argus* signified its approval: "His exertions to establish a theatre in this city have thus far proved successful, and with a good stock company, and several of the profession of acknowledged ability under employment, is nightly attracting a fair share of patronage."[14] Preston picked up where he had left off twelve years ago. Not only did he offer his new public the same range of plays that he had in 1838-39, but he also hired the tragedian J.H. Oxley, who had starred in those productions and who had shared the stage with him on the closing night of his 1839 season. However, Preston's mixture of *Virginius*, *The Iron Chest*, and *Venice Preserved*, with the customary productions of *Hamlet*, *Othello*, *King Lear*, and

Macbeth, did not attract even enough revenue to allow him to paint his renovated walls. He began catering to less-refined tastes with productions of *The Mountain Devil, The Italian Wife's Revenge*, and *The Idiot Witness*; nevertheless, on August 12, the sheriff "put in an appearance and took out the scenery."[15] The Montplaisir Ballet Troupe were allowed to finish their engagement, Donetti's Monkeys played to packed houses for a week (which was more than Preston's actors had been able to do), and then Preston closed down for a month of further "improvements."

The state of Preston's exchequer was only one of two problems he faced in Albany. Unfortunately, he now had competition. The Albany Museum was offering the citizens a more attractive range of productions and more talented performers. Preston's second season, beginning in mid-September, fared poorly. Neither *Hamlet*, nor *The Drunkard*, nor Taylor's trained dogs was sufficiently talented to keep the wolf from the door. While the Albany Museum boasted packed houses, Preston could not afford to advertise his productions in the columns of the local papers. His company (which included the actor his first wife had married on her return from Newfoundland, H.F. Nichols) was adequate but uninteresting. There was little the beleagured manager could do.

The dangers that Preston faced from without—competition and poverty—were dangers he had faced before. The worst menace to both his theatre and his future, unrecognized until it was too late, came from within. Madame Julie de Marguerittes was a force for which all his experience had not prepared him. The deserted wife of a French count, she was making her living in America as an opera singer. She had married George "Gaslight" Foster, author of the now-forgotten *New York Naked*, and she had brought her company to Albany for a short engagement.[16] On October 12, 1852, this redoubtable manager opened her production of Bellini's *La Sonnambula*. It was the beginning of Preston's end.

As usual, Preston's renovations had critically overextended his financial resources. He turned to Madame Marguerittes, and the two managers signed an agreement of partnership in the Albany New Theatre. Almost immediately, Preston found himself ejected from his theatre by his erstwhile partner. The case went before the courts, but while the legal battle was continuing Preston decided on a more direct resolution of the situation. He assembled a gang of fourteen armed men and, in the dawn's early light, stormed what had until recently been his own building.

> The party went immediately to work to bar the doors and windows . . . A posse of the Police was summoned [by Madame de Marguerittes] and on arriving at the private entrance on Hamilton Street, the Madame demanded admittance. This was refused, and death threatened to those who should make the attempt to force open the door; and for the purpose of intimidating the officers, muskets were pointed at them from the windows. The Madame not being admitted, she directed the Police to break open the door which they did; and on their entrance some of the party who were inside fled, while a portion of them attacked the officers . . . When we left the place, the two parties were promenading on the stage. The one was desirous of going on with the rehearsal for the evening performance,and the other said the same was his wish. Both were apparently awaiting the movements of their respective counsel.[17]

Preston's *putsch* failed, and the Madame began her rehearsal for the evening's performance of *Much Ado About Nothing*. Both parties took their cases to the forum of public opinion by way of the *Albany Evening Journal*. Preston admitted that his renovations had exceeded his financial resources and that, as a consequence, he entered into an arrangement with Madame de Marguerittes "who represented herself as possessing ample means and resources to finish the building in the style originally contemplated."[18] His plan had been to repay her from box office profits. Madame Marguerittes argued, in response, that Preston had grossly underestimated the cost of the remaining renovations, had intentionally overestimated the box office potential, and had not told her of the three mortgages on the building.[19] The legal verdict went against Preston, and he lost his last theatre. It was small consolation to him that, less than a month after this off-stage drama, the building was sold out from under Madame Marguerittes by its creditors.

With the loss of the Albany New Theatre in 1853, Preston's theatrical career appears to have ended, although he apparently remained in Albany until his death there on May 3, 1859. His obituary serves as an eloquent summation of the failing thespian's final years:

> An Old Actor Drowned—Henry W. Preston, once a favorite actor wherever he performed, and for some years Manager of

Theatres in this city, was drowned night before last. About 11 p.m. he was on the Dock in the vicinity of the Steamboat Landing, and being asked by an acquaintance if he was going home, replied—"I have no home; the worms have holes to crawl into, but poor men are without houses to rest in." The next instant his acquaintance heard a fall and a splash in the water, and that was the end of the once favorite Preston, who in his younger days had hosts of friends, and deserved them, too. Of late years he had indulged in drink to excess, and was very poor.[20]

The old actor's body was recovered a week later, and a coroner's jury returned a verdict of death by accidental drowning.[21]

Preston's career touched few theatrical heights, and nothing he did changed the nature or the direction of American or Canadian theatre. Accepting nineteenth-century drama as he found it, this actor-manager committed his life to bringing actors and audience together. For his efforts, Preston is remembered only in the most detailed of biographical listings and in uncatalogued folders of drama miscellany. But he earned a better fate. He aided the careers of other actors, he developed audiences for theatre, and he sustained theatrical continuity throughout the painful course of his unrewarded career. Preston's life and hard times deserve the understanding, respect and tribute of his theatrical descendants.

Notes

1. *Morning News,* September 3, 1845.
2. *New Brunswick Courier,* December 6, 1845.
3. *Morning News,* December 10, 1845.
4. *Nova Scotian,* February 23, 1846.
5. *Albany Journal,* November 11, 1846.
6. Odell, V, 299.
7. Dormon, 164.
8. *Free Press,* September 14, 1850.
9. *Free Press,* September 30, 1850.
10. Odell, V, 362.
11. Brown, I, 180.
12. *Gazette,* November 11, 1850.
13. Facts and figures concerning the Green Street Theatre are taken from Henry Dickinson Stone, *Personal Recollections of the Drama*

(1873; reprinted New York: Blom, 1969), 22-25.

14. *Argus,* July 12, 1852.
15. Phelps, 282.
16. Phelps, 282-83, provides a short biographical sketch of Mme de Marguerittes.
17. *Evening Journal,* January 10, 1853.
18. *Evening Journal,* January 13, 1853.
19. *Evening Journal,* February 3, 1853.
20. *Argus and Atlas,* May 5, 1859.
21. *Evening Journal,* May 10, 1859.

Chapter Seven

The lives of Hill, Preston and Freer were certainly not changed by the events of 1845. At most, each might have emerged from the year with an insidious taste for success. But none of the three showed any renewed tendency to believe that a successful life was his to attain. Each had been shaped, over these eleven months, by forces he lacked the power to control, and none had moved closer to controlling such forces. After the events of the spring and summer, each went his own way. Hill kept on as a New Brunswick newspaperman, waging failing battles against Responsible Government and his own self-destruction. Preston continued to found and lose theatres up and down the east coast of America; and Freer made one last grasp for the brass ring of stardom in America, and then slipped quietly into the obscurity of London's tavern theatres. There is no indication that they ever met again, although Freer might have bumped into Preston in New York just before Freer gave up on America and returned to England.

It is difficult to decide whether Hill or Preston exhibited greater determination to ruin himself in his later years. While much in Hill's personality seems contrary, if not contradictory, the most inexplicable side of his nature was his anger and violence. In the intellectual jousting of his editorial columns, Hill was the equal of anyone. As a defender of Tory ideals, he was the model of logical consistency. As a proponent of Orangeism, he was free from the anti-Catholic fanaticism found elsewhere. One of the most obvious qualities of his poetry is its gentleness. But, as politicians besides Lemuel Wilmot were quick to discover, Hill could quickly replace intellectual jousting with vicious and emotional attacks. This anger can be explained in part by his hatred of hypocrisy as he saw it practiced by politicians. But Hill's drinking and the violence to which it led are not explained by the external events of his life. Perhaps his main anger was directed at himself. His marriage had broken up when his wife remained in Maine; his first newspaper had quickly failed; his financial state, as far as it is possible to tell, was always precarious; his political opinions won him more enemies than friends; and all this happened while he was fighting for values which he believed, in his heart, to be right.

Alcohol and violence may have provided refuge against frustration and a sense of personal failure, but they almost ended Hill's association with the *Loyalist*. On February 17, 1846, while he was boarding in Doak's home, Hill physically attacked his partner and various members of his family. Hill characterized the exchange as an "angry altercation . . . which soon led to blows, and in a short time the craven [Doak] was induced to kneel in the most abject manner, and beg for pardon."[1] Doak's account of the event reveals, in almost clinical detail, how violent Hill could be.

> Hill . . . with all the ferocity of a savage, attacked Mr. Doak in the most treacherous manner, (having first bolted the door to prevent interference) and after having beat him until exhausted with his own exertions Mr. Doak, in a gore of blood, fell, or rather rose to his knees and begged, not Hill's pardon, but his own life. His sisters, who had previously retired for the night, hearing the struggle below, came rushing into the room, the door having been previously forced open, and openly attempting to remonstrate with Hill, the cowardly villain with a blow of his fist felled one of them to the floor,and while lying insensible at his feet, the vile wretch kicked her several times with his boot.[2]

An altercation such as this, had it been between Hill and Wilmot, might have been understandable. However, in 1842, it had been Doak who "took Hill out of Gaol in Saint John in a state of utter destitution and wretchedness, paid the debt for which he had been incarcerated, clothed him in decent garments—(a luxury perhaps never before enjoyed by him) and placed him in a respectable situation of editor of [the *Loyalist*]." The partnership had experienced some rough moments during its short life, and the split occasioned by Hill's attack was the fourth break-up attributed by Doak to those "vicious habits" which Hill "had imbibed during a lifetime of dissipation, passed strolling from one part of the world to another, [which] had become too deeply rooted, to be easily eradicated."[3] Yet the long-suffering Doak, guided "by a desire to screen if possible the perpetrator of such diabolical deeds, from not only the penalty of the law, but the odium and censure of an indignant

Public," at first hesitated to sever their connection. Only at the urging of "sympathetic friends" did he approach Hill to draw up a document of dissolution of partnership.[4]

The truth surrounding this event will never be clearly known. According to Doak, Hill wrote the document and signed it in front of a witness on February 23. Hill then kept away from the *Loyalist* office until March 4, when the document was to be published. On that day, Hill frequently came into the *Loyalist* office to read the compositors' copy. Doak, suspicious of his former partner, kept the original document in his coat pocket. Unfortunately for Doak, when his help was needed at the power press, he was obliged to take off his coat. Shortly after, Hill picked up Doak's coat, carried it into the empty office and then, a few minutes later, left the building. When Doak returned, the document of dissolution was missing. The indignant Doak immediately went to a Magistrate for a warrant to arrest Hill. Before it could be issued, Hill took "forcible possession of the [*Loyalist*] office, brandishing his pistols, and threatening to destroy the press, if any man attempted to work." Doak appealed to the forces of law and order, Hill was ejected, and the paper went to press. Hill then "tried hard to raise a force to take possession of the Office, but he has failed in procuring fools enough to attempt it"; he threatened and insulted everyone connected with the *Loyalist*; and he began riding around the city streets with a brace of loaded pistols. This was all too much for the peaceable Doak:

> Matters have really come to a pretty pass, when a contemptible villain like this can set a whole community at defiance—and that too under the immediate eye of the law, he has been twice bound over to keep the Peace—but this has no effect on him— he still continues to threaten lives, and to carry loaded pistols constantly about him, no doubt for the purpose of using them, should a favorable opportunity present itself. Will the paltry amount of the Bonds restore a human life, if taken? —And if taken, will the authorities of the City of Fredericton consider that they have done their duty?

Hill's unwillingness to admit that he had broken with Doak was all the more incomprehensible to his former partner because Hill had, during the previous year, dissolved the partnership twice. On May 22, 1845, Hill wrote and published a notice of dissolution, but changed his mind, stopped the presses, and took the announcement out of the paper. Five months later, he once again signed the articles of dissolution; but within the week, "after many promises of future good conduct," he had again been given editorial management of the *Loyalist*. On the evening immediately in question, February 23, 1846, Hill had, in the presence of witnesses, once again voluntarily dissolved the partnership; he returned the pocket watch he had purchased with company funds, despite Doak's remonstrance that it was his to keep; and he rode off on the company mare in the direction of Woodstock with the avowed intention of never more showing his face in Fredericton. Within half an hour of Hill's dramatic departure, he was found once more, with his boots off, in the *Loyalist* office.

Hill, of course, denied Doak's accusations and, in a letter to the *New Brunswick Reporter*, claimed that he had been "grossly, malignantly, and wantonly slandered" in the columns of the paper which he still considered his own.[5] According to Hill, he had been preparing for bed on the night of the altercation when, having heard a noise below, he went downstairs "and saw Doak in a disgraceful position, which, for the sake of his family whom I sincerely respect, I forbear to mention." Conversation quickly gave way to altercation, and name-calling led to blows. Doak, Hill claimed, knelt and begged for pardon. The fight was not something of which Hill was proud, but "few men can control their passion when once aroused." Reflecting on the incident the next morning, Hill, mindful of the years of friendship the two men had shared, went to Doak's bedside, apologized, and received Doak's forgiveness. It was an emotional moment for Hill: "I am not ashamed to confess that upon the morning . . . when I thought upon our past friendship, and looked upon a few slight marks of the preceding rencontre, I wept over him, as he grasped my hand." In Hill's mind, the incident was finished. A few days later, however, he was surprised to discover that Doak had sworn out a charge of assault and battery against him. Hill was also surprised that Doak would claim to be sole proprietor of the *Loyalist*, thus cheating him out of "several hundreds of pounds." According to Hill, there was no document of dissolution of the partnership.

The former partners found themselves before the courts— "the last grand effort," according to Doak, of the man "we warmed and fed . . . But his fangs are poisonless, and we laugh at his imbecile wrath."[6] Doak's confidence was not misplaced. The judge accepted his argument that, though Hill was editor of the paper, he held that position only as long as Doak wished to employ him. Hill's affidavits to the contrary were not found credible. The defeated Hill initiated a number of other cases against Doak and his fellow employees for ejectment and for assault and battery, but these cases achieved nothing other than the publicizing of Hill's drinking and gambling debts. The long-suffering Doak's patience was at an end:

> He has palmed himself upon us and the public quite long enough; and the time has come in which, with his own hand, he has lifted the veil, and stands exposed in all the hideousness of moral deformity. To his own fate, as he has evoked it, we leave him.[7]

At most, the legal battles had given Doak momentary frustration: the post office would not deliver mail addressed to the *Loyalist*, and, until both former partners signed the requisite receipt, the House of Assembly would not pay the agreed-upon hundred pounds to the paper for covering the sitting of the Legislature. Doak was also forced to suffer less serious irritations:

> When we entered our Box in the lobby of the House of Assembly, on Saturday morning last, we found our ink-stand had been stolen. We were the last person who left the lobby on the previous evening with one exception; a man remained *crouched down* beside the box in a very suspicious manner; we remarked him at the time, and when we found the ink-stand had been stolen, we were not at all surprised, knowing the *pick-pocket propensities* of that individual. His name was not VALLEY!!! We would caution the Public to beware of this man!!![8]

The split between the two men who had shared rooms, work, and even jail seemed permanent. But the separation had not come from their hearts. Doak admitted that he would have forgiven Hill's physical assault but for "the interference of sympathizing friends, who would not so tamely submit to the spilling of human blood without seeking redress." Hill thought that with his apology, on the morning after, the incident had been closed. The artificial enmity could be sustained only so long. By the middle of June, the two men had settled their differences and apologies were exchanged. Hill confessed regret for striking the first blow. Doak admitted that his description of the fight had been somewhat augmented by the stories of others. Their real enemies were their pseudo-friends. But this affair would have been hushed up, and the public never *annoyed* with it, but for the officious interference of pretended friends, and infamous tale-bearers, who, not content with running from one to the other, repeating everything they had heard, with additions and variations, drew largely upon their imaginations for what they considered requisite to give their stories *effect*. It was this which inflamed the passions of either party, and led to subsequent transactions.[9]

The pair apologized to the public for having foisted their spat upon the world at large and, having learned a wholesome lesson, conscientiously pledged that the public would "never again hear of a quarrel between their humble servants."

This quarrel, throughout which Hill considered himself the injured party, displays his inner self more than any other incident between the two friends. His violence, his drinking, his gambling, and his lack of respect not only for others but even for himself all come together in this incident. The *Loyalist* was Hill's right arm in the war against Responsible Government, and his willingness to hazard his journalistic career by breaking with Doak suggests that the devils haunting him were more deeply embedded in his psyche than even his political values. His loaded pistols hint of an inclination toward self-annihilation for which nothing known about his life provides sufficient motivation.

Hill's reinstatement as editor signaled the end of his stay in Fredericton. The same *Loyalist* issue which made public the reconciliation also announced that, in order to be near the commercial centre of the province, Hill and Doak were moving their editorial office back to Saint John. The paper reopened in the port city on July 9, 1846, and the partnership endured until the following April when, by amicable agreement, Hill bought out Doak's right and title to the *Loyalist* and carried on as both editor and proprietor. Hill continued the paper under the title *The Loyalist and Protestant Vindicator* until 1852.[10] In January of that year, he moved the paper once again to Fredericton, but it survived only until the summer. Hill probably remained in Fredericton after the demise of his paper.[11] In 1855, he began to work for John Graham's *Head Quarters*, and it was as a result of an editorial he wrote for this paper in 1856 that Hill suffered his final public humiliation.

Throughout his *Loyalist* years in Fredericton, Hill's editorial voice had been heard loud and strong as he publicly and consistently defended the Monarchy, Protestantism, the Tory position, and the rights of a free press to speak freely and forcefully on questions of public interest. He had dismissed Responsible Government as merely a "Whig scheme." He had sneered at the Catholic Daniel O'Connell as "the leather-lunged vendor of scurrility and anarchy." He had committed his voice and his life to the *ideals* of party politics, but he had obviously been able to engage his enemies on whatever level they felt most at ease. Therefore, as he returned to editorial writing with John Graham's paper, he faced his old political and ideological enemies with unrepentant vigor.

Hill's final years in Fredericton were not characterized by the same exuberant range of public and personal battles that had galvanized his earlier stay in the capital city. The main reason for this was that he now had to share an editorial pulpit. As only one of a group of editorial writers for *Head Quarters*, Hill did not now have the freedom to attack his ideological opponents at will. Yet his final confrontation against his old foes began, in the summer of 1856, with an editorial he wrote for Graham's paper. In it he castigated one Alexander Thompson, of Douglas, for flying a banner which was interpreted as being an American flag. Thompson, either on his own or with the assistance of James Hogg, wrote a public response to Hill. Hogg, the editor of the *New Brunswick Reporter* and a frequent target of Hill's scorn, wrath and derision in his *Loyalist* days, published it. Among other comments, Thompson observed, "It ill becomes an Englishman, like Hill, who must have forsworn his allegiance to his own country when he enlisted in the American service, and who first came to this country a Yankee deserter, to prate about loyalty."[12] While this accusation had been hurled at Hill from various editorial pages in the 1840s, he had always treated it as the sort of unsubstantiated name-calling to be expected in the heat of battle. But now, ten years later, left with little more than his own sense of self-respect, Hill rose to this attack on the integrity of his loyalist principles. He sued both Thompson and Hogg for libel, and his last tilt with the windmills of folly began.

Thompson was an insignificant figure on this battlefield. The war was really between the ardent Toryism of Hill and the more liberal politics of Hogg. In this battle of party and ideology, the issue was not justice, but revenge. One of the strongest and most bitter memories of Hill's enemies was the editorial thrashing Hill had given the proponents of Responsible Government in 1844. In the particular editorial that had roused the Assembly to call Hill and Doak before the bar—that same action which had ended with the Assembly's retreating in ignominious defeat—Hill had excoriated L.A. Wilmot for betraying the conservative principles that had got him elected. Wilmot, then at only the beginning of a stellar political career, had been called a "hound" who had "emerged to poison with his fetid breath the atmosphere of New Brunswick."[13] Presenting himself at court fourteen years after writing those intemperate words about Wilmot, Hill must have felt the foretaste of defeat when he looked to the judicial bench and saw there, presiding, Judge Lemuel Allan Wilmot.

Hill's strategy was straightforward. He explained that "this staff is aimed at me, and the *Head Quarters*, and the party, and such is the effect that if this suit is not made out in my favour, I must leave."[14] Thus Hill filed individual suits against Thompson and Hogg. Thompson and Hogg, writer and publisher of the supposed libel, had to choose between two legal strategies. They could deny responsibility for the attack, or they could attempt to prove that Hill's desertion was common knowledge, and thus that their statement was not libelous. They chose the latter course. The suit against Thompson was quickly dismissed on the grounds that, since no one could find the original letter, no one could prove it had ever been written. By dismissing the case against Thompson, Judge Wilmot had cleared the field for the clash of mighty opposites.[15]

The trial was a collection of truth and perjury. Hogg's lawyer brought in witnesses to swear that they had known Hill in Woodstock; that Hill had first appeared in clothes that they took to be the uniform of an American soldier; that Hill had joked about being an American deserter; and that rumors to this effect had been in general circulation for years. This latter point was the most important. The trial, strictly speaking, was not about whether or not Hill had deserted the American army. The trial was to judge whether Hogg was justified *in publishing* that Hill had deserted. If, during almost twenty years, Hill had not rebutted rumors that he had been an American deserter, then Hogg was justified in printing them. Hill's whole career hinged on rumors, such as those published by Ned Ward, which had found their way into print during his earlier Fredericton years and had not been fully denied by him.

❦ NEW-BRUNSWICK VOLUNTEERS ❧
(Composed shortly after the prospect of a border
warfare, 1839.)

Air—Farmers Boy

COME, come my brave New-Brunswick's sons,
  Who'd scorn your soil to yield;
Sheath, sheath your swords and house your guns,
  For the foe has quit the field;
The Chief of Maine, fearing defeat,
  Like a weathercock he veers,
Nor dares his conscript troops shall meet
  New Brunswick Volunteers.

When braggarts came, both foot and horse,
  And swore they would prevail,
And hold our frontier line by force,
  And stop the Royal Mail,—
Oh! when they thus had made their boast,
  Invading our frontiers,
Who flew like lightning to their post?
  New-Brunswick Volunteers.

Then here's to Goldie's sons of fame,*
  Who came in the hour of need;
And here's to the 36th who came
  In our behalf to bleed;
And here's to Brooks** and his band so true,
  Who to our cause adheres,
From India's Western Isles they flew
  To aid the Volunteers.

And here's to Nova Scotia's Chief,
  And her parliament so bold,
Who proffered us their kind relief—
  Their yeomanry and gold!
And here's to the ruler of this land,—
  We'll give for him three cheers;
Likewise for the chief who did command
  New-Brunswick Volunteers.***

Then pledge a bumper high and deep,
   Our coast again is cleared,—
No widows left in woe to weep,
   And the foe has disappeared.
Should they again invade our shore,
   Our foes shall find their biers,
Or strew it o'er with th' clotted gore
   Of Brunswick Volunteers.

                                        T. Hill

*   Colonel Goldie and the 11th Regiment of Foot.
**   Major Brooks of the 69th Foot.
*** Colonel Maxwell of the 36th Foot.
The Constitutional Lyrist, 60-61.

                    ❧

Hill's lawyer provided witnesses who had lived in Woodstock
but had *never* heard these rumors, who had driven Hill to
Houlton *after* the supposed desertion, who knew *another* Tom
Hill who actually had deserted from the American army, and
who claimed that one of the principal defense witnesses was a
drunk. Other witnesses claimed to have known the plaintiff in
Orono, and swore that not only had Hill never been an
American soldier, but that he had left Maine precisely because
he had been expressing his Royalist sentiments too forcefully
for his own health.
   The trial was, in effect, a trying of Hill's character. Judge
Wilmot allowed discussion of whether or not Hill had referred
to his wife as a "d _____ bitch" and had abandoned her and his
family when he left Maine without them—before telling the
jury to disregard this subject. Hill's personal habits—his
gambling and his drinking—were aired. And in his charge to the
jury Wilmot focused their deliberations on the very area of the
case that justice demanded they ignore.
   This is a very important cause—one which demands at your
hand peculiarly careful deliberation; and why? because,
gentlemen, *party* has been brought into court by the learned
counsel on both sides—party feelings, which should never be
allowed to enter here; for when its poisonous influence
contaminates the fountain of Justice, whose waters should be
pure, then we may bid farewell to the justly boasted freedom

107

which belongs to the administration of British Law. I regret that the attempt should be made, has been made, by the trumpet voice of counsel, to arouse party animosities—which I have buried years ago.[16]

Fortunate indeed for Hill that Wilmot had buried such animosities—for Lemuel Allan Wilmot, years before, in a speech on the Keswick River, had himself pronounced Hill an American deserter.[17]

The long newspaper reports of the trial indicate that what should have been a libel action between Hill—whose editorial columns had so viciously attacked Wilmot—and Hogg—whose editorial columns had supported Wilmot—turned out to be, as Wilmot pointed out with such puritanical innocence, a trial which the victors would regard as a party triumph. In his charge to the jury, Wilmot characterized Hill as merely a "puppet" whose strings were being pulled by party members "behind the scene." In the face of the many inconsistencies uttered, it is difficult to imagine that the trial embodied the sense of British fairness and justice to which the judge paid such lip service. It is more difficult to see why Wilmot, having recognized the need for fairness, did not himself stand aside from the case entirely.

Hill, as expected, lost the case, resigned his position with *Head Quarters*, and removed himself from the editorial and political spotlight of New Brunswick. "I have had many difficulties to contend with—many cowardly, sneaking, and unprincipled enemies," Hill wrote with quiet intensity in his valediction, "but I have found some warm friends, whose kindness to me I can never forget. To each and every one of the latter I now bid a kind farewell."[18] The Woodstock *Journal* published one of the few assessments of Hill's career to be made by his contemporaries:

He has made many political enemies, and perhaps few political friends, but to us, these facts speak much more loudly of his honesty, consistency, sturdy independence, and bluntness of speech, than of anything less estimable . . . There were many things in him of which we could not approve. But we do say that he had some of the best and noblest qualities. He had rare independence of spirit, a truly British heart, downrightness of speech, and consistency, and hearty detestation of meanness and sycophancy. During his long career as a journalist he has preserved a general consistency which is as admirable as it is singular. He commenced a Conservative, he continued a Conservative, and he ends a Conservative.[19]

Many of these sentiments were echoed by Hill's own publisher. Graham acknowledged that his former editor was not without flaw. But, more important than such personal failings, Hill had been, "during the storm as well as the sunshine, the unflinching and consistent advocate of truly British and Conservative principles."[20] Graham hinted, in this same editorial, that Hill's trial had indeed been unfair, and he concluded with the hope that, should fairness reassert itself, Hill would rise once more.

But this was the battle from which Hill did not rise. Perhaps he felt that fairness could not be found in New Brunswick. Perhaps he was too tired. Perhaps the effects of personal excesses had taken too great a toll on his body. (One witness at the trial said he had seen Hill a few years back, but that Hill had changed so much since that he would not have recognized him.) Or perhaps Hill did rise, quietly. The *Carleton Sentinel* and the Fredericton *Reporter* would, two years later in their obituaries, say that Hill was until recently on the *Head Quarters* editorial staff. If this is so, Hill merely became less visible as he continued to wage the long and wearying battles that had engaged his whole being for two very stormy decades.

Hill died two years after that unanimous verdict against him, on October 18, 1860. In the only eulogy published by his former friends and editors, Graham attempted to come to grips with the personal problems that Hill's earlier Fredericton years had illustrated. Passing over the misfortunes and infirmities Hill may have had "in common with other children of nature and genius," Graham wrote of Hill's positive side:

Self-educated, self-introduced, self-supported, he showed what such a character could do in a state of society so unformed as ours. He wrote and printed—(the latter very often with his own hands, as he was also a most able reporter for his own press and others)—prose, poetry, politics, novels, romances, serious and comic exhibitions of his views on all the questions of the passing day; and, whatever might be thought or said of his productions by those whom they variously affected, they were distinguished by this one sterling feature, which we cannot but think that even the most exasperated of his antagonists would now concede due honor—principle.[21]

The one other man close to Hill in his final years was his fellow

Head Quarters editor, Richard Phillips. His summation of Hill was closely akin to Graham's in its recognition that Hill was a man of genius. "During his life he proved himself to be one of the most extraordinary men of the age, possessing a giant intellect, independent spirit and a daring and firmness of will that neither neglect, misfortune, privation, nor persecution could subvert."[22]

When Tom Hill died in October, 1860, the process of his devolution into the footnotes of New Brunswick history was already beginning. There were no attempts, beyond those of his fellow editors, to set Hill's life into the larger context of his times. Unfortunately, he had been on the losing side of the main issue of his day, the issue of Responsible Government. History, dealing unkindly with losers, has left whatever role Hill's criticism had in shaping even his opponents' positions on this and other issues largely unexplored. One of the very few writers who would later attempt to sustain Hill's memory was W.G. MacFarlane. Assessing the place of the nearly-forgotten Hill in the context of the mid-1850s, MacFarlane wrote that Hill "distinguished himself as a writer of genius . . . as an ardent tory, Orangeman and Imperial Federationist . . . as a man of power in politics and journalism, and as a poet of considerable ability."[23] Nothing of substance has been written of Hill since these 1895 remarks. Nothing has ever been written of his prose, his poetry, or his one troublesome play.

For Thomas Hill, principle was infinitely more important than the political game. In 1858, reporting on his own trial, he said of himself (in the editorial third person) that "if he had one ruling passion stronger than another it was his love for his country, veneration for her laws and institutions, and pride in the glory of the Empire."[24] This declaration might have furnished his epitaph. Unfortunately, as he died penniless and almost friendless, there was no tombstone on which to record such sentiments or even the simple fact that he had lived.

In his last years, Charles Freer had felt himself drawn back to the theatrical outskirts of his former east-end triumphs, as though memories could provide the starving actor with consolation for his lost talents. Henry W. Preston, exhausted in body and despondent in mind, remained to die in Albany, where ghosts of treachery and final defeat must have been smothered by memories of his successful seasons. Both men had been drawn to lives of theatrical wandering, and, in their final declines, both were drawn back to the scenes of their greatest triumphs, as though physical closeness to the cold bricks of the theatres which now rejected them could somehow substitute for the warmth of home and hearth. Hill, as rootless as they, chóse to suffer his own decline in the city of his most glorious victories. In that same city, where he had faced down the House of Assembly, and Ned Ward, and Lemuel Allen Wilmot, and James Hogg, and his many other opponents, his body was laid in the family plot of one of his two remaining friends—John Graham.[25] The only other mourner was Richard Phillips. Little notice was taken of his sudden passing. However, as he lay on his deathbed, all but ignored by the province for which he had waged such mighty battles, an earthquake shook New Brunswick and Maine—a shaking of such force that his death was marked by the unintended slow tolling of steeple bells over the many churches in which he had never set foot. It was the sort of irony that Tom Hill would have been quick to appreciate.

ϫ *FARE THEE WELL* ϫ

French Air

FARE thee well land of my birth,
  Dear unto me ever,
Not an object on this earth
  My heart from thee shall sever.

Chorus: Charming were thy flowery dells
      When last I gazed upon thee;
      Sweetly rung the village bells
      When fortune tore me from thee.

Fare thee well my childhood's home,
  Where long I dwelt so blithely;
Though destined far from thee to roam,
  I'll dream upon thee nightly.

Can I forget—while Flora's beam
  Came glimmering down the alley—

How oft I've wandered by the stream
  Which decks thy rural valley!

Can I forget that ancient pile
  With gothic shire and sashes,
While sleeps in the surrounding soil
  My friends'—my mother's ashes!

The friends from whom I wept to part—
  Whom still I love most dearly—
Thou still retains with them my heart,
  And life from thee how dreary!

Those evening bells—how dear the sound—
  How oft with childish wonder,
I've listened to the cheering round
  Awakening echo's thunder.

One lonely wish my bosom draws—
  From foreign lands to sally;
Once more the raging main to cross,
  And see my native valley.

        Charming were thy flowery dells
          When last I gazed upon thee;
        Sweetly rung the village bells
          When fortune tore me from thee.

                    T. Hill

The Constitutional Lyrist, 233-34.

Notes

1. Hill's account of this incident is recorded in the *New Brunswick Reporter*, March 5, 1846.
2. *Loyalist*, March 12, 1846.
3. *Loyalist*, March 12, 1846.
4. Doak's response to, and accounts of, the happenings surrounding this incident are to be found in the *Loyalist*, March 5 and 12, 1846.
5. Hill's account of the events was published in the *New Brunswick Reporter*, March 6, 1846.
6. *Loyalist*, March 26, 1846.
7. *Loyalist*, March 26, 1846.
8. *Loyalist*, April 9, 1846.
9. *Loyalist*, June 18, 1846.
10. Harper, 68. I have not seen any of these issues of the paper. They are not included on the *Loyalist* microfilm provided by Mount Allison University.
11. The Fredericton Magistrates Court records for March 25, 1853 (Archives, Harriet Irving Library, MGH46), show that Hill paid the debt of William McKnight. Harper, 25, indicates that Hill published *The United Empire* from May to August, 1854, in Fredericton.
12. *New Brunswick Reporter*, July 11, 1856.
13. *Loyalist*, February 23, 1844.
14. *New Brunswick Reporter*, March 12, 1858. Note that while Hill's editorial was written in 1856, the case came to trial only in 1858.
15. For accounts of the trial, see Chapter One, n. 1, p. 00.
16. *Carleton Sentinel*, March 6, 1858.
17. *Head Quarters*, March 24, 1858.
18. *Head Quarters*, March 3, 1858.
19. Quoted in *Head Quarters*, March 17, 1858.
20. *Head Quarters*, March 17, 1858.
21. *Head Quarters*, October 24, 1860.
22. Quoted in W.G. MacFarlane, *New Brunswick Bibliography* (Saint John: Sun Printing Company, 1895), 44.
23. MacFarlane, 44.
24. *Head Quarters*, March 24, 1858.
25. Louise Hill, *The Old Burying Ground: Fredericton N.B.* (Fredericton: distributed by Fredericton Heritage Trust, 1981), I, 38-39.